Peter Pravica

About the Author

GEORGE ENGLUND, seventy-nine, is a writer, producer, and director. He directed Marlon Brando in the 1963 film *The Ugly American*. He lives in Palm Springs, California, with his dog, Eli.

I was directing Marlon in a scene in *The Ugly American* and he was not delivering the performance we both wanted, both knew he was capable of. We had done six takes, and when I said, "Cut," after the seventh, he still had not succeeded.

"I know what you want," Marlon said. "I don't know what's keeping me from getting it."

He paused for a long moment then looked up. "You know what it is, I just don't want to do it the way it's ever been done before."

That was Marlon to the core. Where most actors would be trying to excel at playing a scene the conventional way, the way it had so often been played before, he would be searching in another dell of human life, wanting to be original, astonishing.

I thought at the moment he said those words they should be a rallying cry for all actors and artists. It seems to me now that the words say every bit as much about Marlon's life as they do about his art.

MARLON BRANDO

The Way It's Never
Been Done Before

George Englund

Harper

An Imprint of HarperCollins*Publishers*

PHOTOGRAPHIC CREDITS Pages xii, 28, 90, 108, 118, 152, 226, 240, 276: AP/Wide World Photos; 56, 70, 138, 184, 260: personal collection of George Englund; iv, 206: Herman Leonard (photographer).

Previously published in hardcover as *The Way It's Never Been Done Before: My Friendship with Marlon Brando* in 2004 by HarperEntertainment, an imprint of HarperCollins Publishers.

First Harper paperback published 2005.

Designed by JoAnn Metsch

Library of Congress Cataloging-in-Publication Data is available upon request.

ISBN 0-06-078630-2
ISBN-10: 0-06-083286-X (pbk.)
ISBN-13: 978-0-06-083286-5 (pbk.)

05   06   07   08   09   ❖/RRD   10   9   8   7   6   5   4   3   2   1

Sometimes when we walked in the gloaming, other times when we were charged with anger, but ubiquitously, persistently, Marlon and I talked about our fathers. Only rarely did our mothers come into our conversations. And yet, as I look back on the paths our lives followed, I see how much our directions, our questings, were shaped by our mothers.

With every passing day I sense more deeply my mother's hand on my life. Marlon's mother was too often lost to him, too often in an alcoholic mist outside his reach, but her maternal force was in him.

Though physically Marlon took much from the confused, gnarly man who was his father, that man was plainly not the source of Marlon's talent. I believe the source was his mother.

So I dedicate this book to two redoubtable women, Dorothy and Mabel, actresses both, gentle women both. A salute to the girls they were in their twenties when they gave birth to us, a wave of gratitude for the humor and love of laughter they bestowed on us. I know Marlon would join me in saying, "Take a bow, Mom, your son is grateful to you."

Author's Note

More than once over the years Marlon said, "I want you to write something, Georgie, sit down and write a book."

"I'm not sure what I'd write about, Mar," I'd respond.

"Write about anything, write about something you know."

I didn't write that book about something I know, I wrote this one about *somebody* I know. I didn't discuss the book with Marlon, I planned to give it to him when it was finished. I planned that he would write a foreword.

In early 2004, when I realized Marlon's condition was not likely to improve, I began to assemble the book in earnest. I thought that when he died, along with the cascade of praise and superlatives that would be showered on him, there should be a personal book about Marlon, a book by someone who knew him well.

It would be a daunting task to capture the iridescence of Marlon, to see life through the prism of his mind, but I thought I should attempt it. I began an odyssey into the past. As I traveled there, I saw our sails between the waves, heard our boyish, bawdy laughter, remembered somber times when we were both seized with anxiety, two birds flying over the dark sea, no land in sight. I revisited the cities—of the earth and the mind—where Marlon and I spent time. I relived the abuse we perpetrated on our friendship and the grandeur we often added to it. We shared parties, gave support through our marriages, grieved over our children, let each other inside where no one else ever was allowed. We sailed under full top gallants, not noticing time.

I have noticed it now.

There is one last thing to say. When Marlon and I first became friends, he was deeply interested in how important it was to me to be right. It was important; I'd gone to military school and been in the navy and learned that if you took a position on something, you'd better be able to support it. But Marlon wasn't talking about that; he was peering into the emotional side of me, seeing that I felt insecure and possibly unmanned if something I said turned out to be wrong.

His idea was to be naked, absolutely present to whatever emotion came—fear, humiliation, insecurity, anything. If I felt fear, be truthful about it; if I felt humiliation, allow it to be there, don't mask it.

That teaching from Marlon has proved to be a gift of the highest value. In this book I have tried to be faithful to Marlon's way, I have tried to see us naked, to describe both of us as we are.

July 2004

MARLON BRANDO

I

—

M*February 16, 2004*
arlon is an old man. I both laugh and weep as I write the sentence. Marlon old? Marlon Brando old? It can't be true. It is, though; he's eighty. But it isn't the number of years that's significant, Marlon could still be youthful. It's how the years have treated him and how he has treated them. And he isn't old to me, we still fire the jokes and puns back and forth, still kid and prod each other, still rail at what's loathsome on television, still read our favorite poems aloud. *The Ballad of William Sycamore* by Stephen Vincent Benét is a perennial.

But age is here. Today, when I walk down the hall to Marlon's bedroom, on the polished teak that has supported my shoes through so many crossings, I hear it, faintly at first, then more certainly as I near the entrance—the hiss of the oxygen tank. When I cross into the bedroom–sitting area, it's quiet, there is an unaccustomed stillness, I am in the whereabouts of an old man. The appurtenances of illness—bottles of pills, boxes of medications, syringes, lotions and lubricants—fill the surface of the bedside table and tell a story of infirmity. And in his bed Marlon's mien is that of a man who is not well.

It is midday, I have driven from Palm Springs. Marlon and I will have lunch, talk for a while, then I'll put my things in the guesthouse down below the swimming pool while he rests. At some point I will discuss with him the project he began three years ago that he first called *Master Class* then later *Lying for a Living*. Marlon meant it to be a top-secret, clandestine endeavor, but, of course, news of it soon landed in the press. He brought a group of actors together, some completely unknown, others established stars—Nick Nolte, Robin Williams, Whoopi Goldberg, Sean Penn, Leonardo DiCaprio, Jon Voight, Michael Jackson. Marlon instructed them in the use of improvisation in acting, then had them perform improvisations. He hired the controversial English director Tony Kaye to record the sessions on DVD and almost immediately had a falling-out with him and fired him.

He believes the project will bring him scores of millions of dollars. I believe there can be money in what Marlon has to teach about acting, but the madness that prevails when he controls the business side as well as the creative side of a project will likely prevent his work from reaching the audience it might.

His theme is that acting is lying and that this notion should first be brought to the attention of politicians.

"Politicians lie all the time, that's their principal occupation, but they don't do it well. I can teach them how to lie with style," he says.

After the material had been assembled, Marlon asked me to look at it. We then had a protracted discussion about the DVDs and he asked me to take over the whole enterprise, the legal structure, editing the footage into a salable package, creating and executing the marketing and sales campaign. Also, he wanted me to appear with him on the DVD and lead him into a wide-ranging discussion of the kind we have so often. Finally, he wanted me to appear alone talking about him as man and actor.

I am anxious that this project be completed; I feel it is essential that Marlon not leave this planet without, in some form, having set down his view of acting—what acting is and how the art should be approached and rendered.

We agreed on what my responsibilities would be, specifically the duties listed above, then, as happened so often and so amusingly with us, we did not agree on what I should be paid. That brought a schism. After I thought about it, I told Marlon that at this point in life what was important was our friendship, I'd do the job as his friend, without compensation. It's critical, I said, that we build on what's been recorded and create a Brando legacy.

"Good to see you, Georgie." Marlon gestures at me. "Look good. Feeling strong?"

"Ready to run the four-forty, Mar, what about you?"

"Not bad, when I get out of bed I roll my oxygen tank around like a beach ball, that's good exercise. What do you want for lunch?"

Angela, the sweet thirty-four-year-old Filipina, who began as Marlon's maid a few years ago and now takes care of all of the details of his life, is nearby and looking at me with a smile. Her sister stands alongside to assist.

"Anything, Mar, I'm easy, maybe just some Rosicrucian fennel cakes."

"I don't know if we have those," Angela says ingenuously.

"He's bullshitting," Marlon tells her with a laugh, but he has to build on the idea. "You like them sautéed, right, shredded camel dung on top?"

"These days I'm leaning to walrus phlegm, for tartness."

"He'll have what I'm having." Marlon nods to Angela.

"Mr. Brando is having tuna salad, is that what you'd like?" She smiles at me. "We've got other choices."

"Tuna salad." Marlon looks up at her. "He's not able to say it, but he wants tuna salad."

Angela smiles again. "What would you like to drink?"

"Whatever Marlon thinks goes best with fennel cakes."

"Iced tea," he says to Angela. "We'll both have iced tea."

Angela leaves.

In this house on Mulholland Drive, which overlooks Beverly Hills on one side and the San Fernando Valley on the other, and in which Marlon has lived for over forty years, we are in our customary positions—Marlon in bed, I in the chair facing him. Less than a year ago Marlon, who is five-ten, weighed in excess of three hundred and fifty pounds. In the past, he'd made forays into dieting, mostly without conviction, but eleven months ago, when he was having trouble breathing because all that weight had been pressing on his heart, lungs, and central organs for decades, the word from his doctors was an imperative. You must lose weight, Marlon, this condition can kill you.

He began a diet mostly, it seemed to me, of his own creation. That was the genuine Marlon, he would not do it the conventional way, he abhorred the expected, the predictable—

in acting, in social behavior, in politics, in everything. So when it came to dieting, the activity in which eighty percent of America is involved, he shunned the known ways.

Like a medieval alchemist, he pulled the granules of facts to his tabletop, pored over them, peered at them, held them up to the light, rubbed them on his sleeve, then sat back and contemplated how he would synthesize them. Where the alchemist emerged with a new formula for making gold, Marlon returned from his sequestration with a new orthodoxy for losing weight.

His regimen called mainly for assorted greens with lemon juice accompaniment, and, alone on a plate, a bit of fish that had been cooked in some nonbutter-nonoil-non-anything-that-would-make-it-taste-good way. The diet was both effective and a torture to his body, he lost his appetite completely, he couldn't eat. In too short a time he shed sixty-five or seventy pounds. He was weak, his muscle tone was nearly gone, his loosened flesh yielded to the pull of gravity.

"How's Stretch?" Marlon asks.

He's talking about my son, Graves, who's eighteen and a freshman at the University of Georgia. He's six-five.

"Excellent, but all too quickly, Mar, he's a grown-up. I've switched from parent to adviser."

"Wonderful kid."

"He left a cavity when he went off. What about you, Mar, anything I can do to be helpful?"

"Nothing, Georgie, Angela takes care of everything. Your coming up, spending a little time, is plenty."

"I'm full of energy, let me know."

"You're full of energy and I'm full of piss," he says. He pulls the sheet and blanket back, turns on his right side, fits his dick into a flasklike receptacle, and pees. He either doesn't want to or doesn't have the energy to walk to the bathroom and stand for the long time it would take to empty his bladder.

B right sunlight strikes my eyes and a video of another time runs in my mind. It's 1955, after Marlon won an Oscar for *On the Waterfront* and a few months after Marlon and I first met. Cloris Leachman, to whom I was then married, Rita Moreno, and Marlon and I are at the beach together. Marlon's thunder rolls through the movie industry, he's the most formidable star ever, so going to a public beach is a mad idea. Even so, we've come to Santa Monica, where I played two-man volleyball all through college. If Marlon is recognized there will be a mass swarming, but we've decided to chance it. We've walked up the beach to where the crowd is sparse and he and I can toss a football. We throw short, tight spirals then long, arching passes so the other has to dive into the waves to catch the ball. It's the first time Marlon and I have been together out of civilian clothes, the first time we've gotten a look at each other's athletic abilities. We are both skilled. Guys who have been involved in sports all their lives find out about one another early. We're showing our best stuff, pump, fake, then throw in the other direction, run a slant pattern, and make the diving catch.

Out of that day I remember most how Marlon looked. I've been around athletics all my life and seen a lot of well-trained bodies. I don't think I've ever seen one quite like Marlon's. He was finely developed everywhere, abdomen flat and etched,

legs powerful and in symmetry. Upper body strongly mus-
cled, well defined. Yet, with that heavy musculature, he ran,
feinted, and cut with forest-animal swiftness.

I remembered how I'd hoped, as the years went by and Marlon became heavier, that he would drop the weight and come
back to that extraordinary physical form, that he'd saunter
among us again with the old éclat, the rake's smile, the sex,
that giant acting engine revving inside him. He could have
done it; back then Marlon could outlast anyone or anything.
But as he became more and more a power in the industry and
could have just about anyone or anything he wanted, his self-
discipline, and the sense that sometime he would need it,
began to diminish.

Today the young man with the glorious body is in bed here,
drained, tired, weak from his coughing. Oxygen cords lie at
the base of each nostril. His principal problem is idiopul-
monary syndrome, which means, he has told me, a hardening
in the bottom of the lungs, cause unknown. It's the illness his
sister Franny died from ten years ago.

As we talk, Marlon's thoughts are quick and his instant
associations sparkle, but his thinking avenues have narrowed.
Bias and black-and-white judgments are his mental helmsmen
now. Most of all, suspicion, that slithering snake that has
always lived inside him, is untethered, and, like Cardinal
Richelieu bending to his sovereign's ear, guides Marlon's
behavior with everyone he meets.

He begins to discourse on a recurrent theme. "I've found
my way to peace, Georgie, at last; I'm not judgmental any-

more, I've learned to accept others as they are. I understand Titty"—his sister Jocelyn—"got no more conflict there, and I understand that ex-wives have to be ex-wives, okay, let them do what they have to do. And the friends I felt betrayed me, I don't resent them anymore, thank God I've come to this maturity." We sit silently a moment and he slips into a familiar rant—about his former maid-turned-lover and mother of his three youngest known children, now aged fourteen, twelve, and nine. "Christina tried to sue me for a hundred million dollars, pathetic, she gets some asshole greedy lawyer, they try to get me into court . . ."

And quickly we are off the Buddha-like acceptance of the shortcomings of others.

"I read about it," I say. "Is the suit going anywhere?"

"It's bullshit, they wound up getting nothing." Another pause. "This guy wants to run day tours from Tahiti over to Tetiaroa."

"Sounds like a good idea."

"Sure it's a good idea, it's my idea, I started it years ago, but the operation fell apart, it needs to be better organized, this guy's got the boats to bring the people over."

"Good, that would give you a new revenue source. Is he established, do you know him?"

"He wants too much money," Marlon says, "too big a slice, he wants to own the operation."

"That could be good, you get so much a head and have no responsibilities, you wouldn't have to worry about insurance, maintenance, all that."

"We'll see. But the guy's always going to want too much, I see him coming." Marlon frowns. "He's not going to get anywhere trying to fuck with me."

"You ought to get your lawyer into it, see if he can work out a deal," I offer. "Those day tours could fade some of your overhead."

Marlon takes a long breath. "I'll keep talking to the guy, wait till he hangs himself."

When Marlon became a movie star of such titanic proportions, the suspicion that was natively in him swelled. Everybody wants something from a movie star—an autograph, money, to be his agent, to be his friend, to be his lover. It's all massively insincere, so at that point in Marlon's life, deep, wholesale suspicion of every person that came his way was not only justified but required. That intense suspicion has been with him ever since.

There are three pills laid out on the bedside table; he picks them up, tosses them into his mouth, and with a swallow of water sends them down. I ask myself if I am watching Marlon come to the end of his life. Over the past weeks we've talked about his cures and therapies, that there are hopeful signs, he can get by with less oxygen, but we haven't drilled down into the core of the subject, we haven't talked about whether he's dying. We will, soon. After a lifetime of sharing thoughts on every subject, we will not shrink from this one. I laugh inwardly that Marlon so hates being predictable that he might *will* himself to live to be a hundred and eight. Then there's the simple randomness of life, which says it's by no means certain he'll die before I do. Death has often been a subject we've sat with; the deaths of his mother and father, his daughter, my two sons. We have walked deep into the cavern. One night, ages ago, on that tiny little speck that troubles the surface of the south Pacific, Marlon's atoll, Tetiaroa, we talked about death.

Tetiaroa lies forty miles off Tahiti. It is part of the Tuamotu Archipelago in French Polynesia. An atoll is a ring-shaped coral reef that encloses a lagoon; Marlon's atoll is about a mile in diameter. In a handwritten letter to me in 1966 he wrote:

Dear George,

Got in last night, tired and tense from trying to be grown-up. I've been traveling far and near, in and around the islands, under the wind trying to find land and a way to live that allows me to be simpler than these recent years and circumstances have allowed. I bought a 50-foot yacht, a motor sailer, $26,000, and am closing a deal on a coral atoll for $200,000, thirteen islands in all so the fat's in the fire now.

The sand-covered coral masses in the lagoon rise only a few feet above the water. Vessels cannot enter because of the coral reef, but the entirety of ocean life flows through, from sixteen-foot sharks to tiny mollusks. Marlon is intimate with this life. He'll lie down next to a column of hermit crabs that are laboriously carrying bits of driftwood along the shore, study them intently, then begin to imitate them.

Marlon has spent long hours in the ruins of the huts of the Polynesians who once lived and danced here; he knows that like them he'll soon be gone. Leaving what? The thought absorbs him. He doesn't own Tetiaroa, he says, he has it on loan. He's preserved the atoll in its natural state and he'd like his children to be moved by Tetiaroa's sacredness as he is, and to keep it sacred after he's gone. They don't seem to share his interest. He is sometimes preoccupied with what will happen after his death. He doesn't like to think about it, but occasionally we do discuss the fate of the atoll.

He hasn't been to Tetiaroa in several years. First, the parents of Dag Drollet, the young man Marlon's son Christian killed in Marlon's house, have sued Marlon as being partly responsible for their son's death. It would be dangerous for Marlon to go back and face that charge. Then his daughter Cheyenne committed suicide in Tahiti; that shattered him, and he has been unable to stand on the place where it happened.

On Tetiaroa you live in a thatch-topped bungalow called a fare, no blankets, no air-conditioning—the trade winds play through it day and night. You wear shorts or a sarong, swim in the lagoon, snorkel, read, rest, join whoever else is there for dinner.

Lie on your back at night and the pageant you see is limitless, no hills or skyline intrude, there is nothing man-made or noisy near you, there is no other light. There is only the feel of soft wind and in the distance faint booms from the ocean butting against the coral reef. The stars in that dark immensity are vivid and close. An odd sensation comes: you feel you are not still, you are in motion, a traveler through this starry vitality. You understand Stonehenge and Druid priests, shamans creating ceremonies, erecting obelisks, Mayans making human sacrifices because some response had to be made to this infinitude, some shout had to come up from us to it. You understand why we invent constellations, the Big Dipper, the Little Dipper, Orion and his dog, the Seven Sisters. It's to find friendliness out there, to believe this extravaganza of planets and muons and black holes and quarks in some way has an interest in us, that it somehow understands the impor-

tance of our teeny planet in a backwater solar system whose
creatures assault one another to give their lives significance.

When you are alone on the atoll at night, the door in you
swings out to the universe and through it enter the thoughts
you meant someday to spend time with but which, for most
of your life, have lain covered over in your everyday. Who are
you? What should you do while you live?

Marlon offers you this place in which to feel, to imagine
and wonder. No peyote, no dope, but mind-altering, yes. He
gives you the galaxies out there and the hermit crabs at your
feet; somewhere in between is your place. You have the
opportunity to think about your place, perhaps to find it. You
have the opportunity to stop for a real conversation with that
creature you encounter so often on Tetiaroa—yourself.

One night as we lay side by side looking up, we got on the
subject of death.

"Fuck death," Marlon has just said. "I'm not afraid of it."
And at that moment when death seems such a distant concept, I'm sure he isn't. The picture in my mind is that when
Marlon sees death approaching, that ferocious curiosity in
him will rise up to meet it. He will want to hold death's face
as it descends toward him, want to know more even as he
hears the final fluttering of his heart.

"Out here in the middle of the ocean, it's hard to believe
that death is important, even that life is," I say.

"Of course it's not important," Marlon responds. "If both
of us died tonight, would there be one less ripple in the
lagoon, would the trade winds pause, would one blue-footed
booby run and tell the others? It's frightening to people that
their lives have no importance, so they invent some. Put your
kids through college, write a will, protect the environment,

be on time for your Elks meetings. And when it's all done be sure not to notice that not one iota of it mattered. Look out there." He gestures to the night sky. "You can see how indifferent the universe is to anything we do, whether it's helping an old lady across the street or blowing off an atom bomb . . . our life is meaningless yet we're scared to death of death."

"I remember how scary it was when I first got the concept of death," I say. "I was four, my sister and two friends and I were playing in front of our apartment building in Lynn, Massachusetts. One of them said the old man on the fourth floor had died. The black car parked near us was going to take him away.

" 'What is died?' I asked.

" 'Died is death, you get very sick and you have bandages all over and they take you away.'

" 'Where?' I asked.

" 'I don't know, somewhere.'

" 'Will the old man come back?' I was beginning to be frightened.

" 'No, you don't ever come back.'

"The information fit with graceful horror into my fear that I wasn't secured to anybody. Now came this menace, at some point in life I'd be taken away by strangers."

"Gets back to not having a father," Marlon says. "That's where those feelings come from. Nobody gave you security."

"Every once in a while I get a glimpse of how different my life would have been if I'd had a father."

"It wouldn't have solved anything, you'd have had other problems," Marlon replies. "I had a father and I felt almost nothing but anger toward him, sometimes I hated him."

"I see why you were angry at your father, but I don't think

you realize he had a great value just because he was there. Even if you hated him he was the North Pole."

"He wasn't a pole, he wasn't anything. You've got this ideal picture of a father, a two-year-old's picture. Look what happened when you finally met your father, he didn't give you anything. You should have shot him."

There is grace in the small pageant I'm watching. The women are attending to Marlon's needs, ordering the objects on the night table, straightening the bedclothes, administering pills, locating the TV remote—it's normal, it's the cosseting we supply to the one going down the road to death. But when death comes, when this bed is no longer Marlon's sanctuary but has become his catafalque, this version of normalcy will end swiftly. The aftermath will not be as any of us imagined. Grief in its pure form, heavy, somber, laden with dark mysteries, will fill our living space.

Marlon is talking now about a letter I sent to him thirty-five years ago. "I memorized that letter, Georgie, I can't tell you how much pleasure I've gotten from it, I laugh out loud every time I read it . . . so often I pull it out and look at it again."

His mind roams to other times, where we were, with whom we were, how we laughed with them and about them. He recalls Rupert Stillworth-Manley, who was one of our liaison officers at the United Nations when we were doing the research that led to the making of *The Ugly American*. Stillworth-Manley was middle-aged, a traditional and typical

English civil servant with the classic facial gymnastics. He raised his upper lip frequently to reveal a record-breaking case of gum recession and a tangle of teeth; he affected a stutter and showed a fawning enthusiasm for any ideas suggested by his superiors. He bathed too infrequently and somehow Marlon conveys that in the imitation he is doing here and now.

"Well, you could, you know," Marlon says as Stillworth-Manley, "just, just, just turn it round, start at India and work your way east to the Philippines, I mean, why, why not, jolly good thinking it-it-it seems to me.

"Can you imagine having teeth like that?" Marlon says. "Only the British don't know that teeth are part of cosmetics." He pauses thoughtfully. "Do you think Stillworth-Manley could have been married? How would he get to it?

"Angela, dear." He's Stillworth-Manley again. "I do think I love you, I feel so strongly for you.

"But, Rupert," Marlon continues as Angela, "your . . . I can hardly say the word, your teeth, good God, who could sit across from that dental hell every night?

"But, dearest, couldn't I kiss you to-to-to show how much I love you?

"Rupert, not in this life can I forgive you for putting that picture in my mind."

Stillworth-Manley may be dead by now, no matter, he is back for a brilliant reprise in Marlon's bedroom.

"Remember that night we drove up the coast and that guy tried to bust us," Marlon says after a pause.

"Like it was yesterday," I say, and it is true.

"Jesus, we were on fire in those days, was there any subject we didn't cover?"

It was one of those nights in our early years when there wasn't enough time to say all we wanted to tell each other— about politics, acting, love, the electric power in eels, medical advances, robotics, neurotics, psychotics.

We'd had dinner at a restaurant in the valley then driven up the coast beyond Oxnard. I don't remember why but Marlon was driving a rented sedan. At around midnight we were back in Santa Monica but still not talked out, so Marlon turned into one of the parking lots along the beach. He pulled out to the edge where we could see the surf, and killed the lights and the engine. He was telling me how he'd gotten his nose broken while he was starring in *A Streetcar Named Desire* on Broadway.

"This stagehand, Eddie, nice kid, good friend, he and I both liked to box, so we'd spar around between acts. It got pretty animated sometimes and this one night I ducked his jab and was about to land an uppercut when I walked right into a follow-up punch."

A black-and-white prowl car turned into the lot. It hesitated as the cop surveyed the area. The car turned our way. It was at Marlon's back, he didn't see it. It pulled up behind us. Now Marlon was aware of the headlights.

"Cop," I said.

Marlon went on talking with no variation in speed, no adjustment in body position. "There's blood everywhere, I'm a gushing fountain, and it's in the middle of the performance, so they have to see if I can possibly do the last act. They laid me down with my feet up to try to stop the bleeding."

The cop got out of his car with his long silver flashlight and began the measured stroll to us. He shined the light in our back window as he walked. Marlon didn't react. The policeman was at his door, he shined the flashlight on the back of Marlon's head. Again Marlon didn't respond.

"They stuffed cotton up my nose and I don't know what else, somehow I get through the act. Right after the curtain, the producer, Cheryl Crawford, Ernie the stage manager, the investors, everybody rushed me to the hospital."

The cop shined the flashlight on me. I didn't react. He didn't like that, the atmosphere was starting to be menacing. Caparisoned in its red and blue lights, its badges, bullets, and black clothes, Authority had arrived. This was its territory; it made the rules and it enforced them. Marlon would introduce a different perspective. He doesn't know your rules, and if he does he doesn't give a shit about them. And that goes if you're the president, the prime minister, or the policeman in the prowl car.

The cop shined the light on Marlon again. Marlon's back was to the cop, he was facing me and talking to me.

"I'd been doing the show for a year straight and I really needed some time off, so at the hospital I did my best acting as a guy who was losing the power of speech from a broken nose, 'Oh God, my nose, I can't breathe . . . ' "

The cop was pissed, people were supposed to be intimidated by the flashlight. But not this guy. The cop rapped on Marlon's window. Marlon didn't move.

The officer's face knit, he was finding neither anger nor contrition. He knew anger, the guys he rousted in the middle of a hump, and he knew contrition, the ashen ones who believed that knowledge of every sin they'd ever committed was in this cop's hands. He rapped again, hard.

"Let's get that window rolled down."

Without turning, Marlon reached across his body with his right hand and pushed the electric window lever. His window descended. A quarter of an inch.

Naked insolence, stick your flashlight up your ass.

The cop had two choices, both of them loaded with humiliation—he could yell through the window or put his face up and talk through the crack. He took the second option, moved up, and talked through the crack.

"Let's get a look at your license in there."

His eyes were above the window so he whipped his head down to see. It was part Kafka, part Molière, in under a minute, without saying a word, Marlon had this man playing a nutty version of Simon Says. Marlon took his license out of his wallet and slid it up the window to the crack. He used the tips of his fingers to push it through. The officer made a claw on the other side to grasp it. He shined his flashlight on the license and the name bounced to his eyes, Marlon Brando. A Stan Laurel smile broke out.

"Mr. Brando. Marlon Brando?"

There was a higher note in his voice as he metamorphosed from alpha male to movie-star fan. Hey, this wasn't just a movie star, this was *the* movie star, the huge one, the mysterious guy. The cop put the license in front of the flashlight again. The name was there. He held the license out to the window to return it. Marlon was nerveless, as unimpressed with the cop's amity as with his hostility. He lowered the window and took the license. The cop leaned forward.

"Didn't mean to disturb you, Mr. Brando. But if we see two males in a parked car, our orders are to check it out."

"What are you checking out?"

"Homosexual conduct. I'll give my wife a laugh when I tell her I asked Zapata if he was involved in homosexual conduct. No ticket, Mr. Brando, but it will be big news at the station if I get your autograph." He held out his citation pad and a pen. "Would you mind?"

"Okay."

"Seen all your pictures, in *Zapata!* you looked more Mexican than Rodriguez got the locker next to me."

"What do you do if you find two males having sex?" Marlon asked.

"Depends. If they're way out of line or if they get rough, we run them in."

"Fags get rough sometimes?" He had written his name and was adding curlicues.

"Better believe it. I had to call for backup once."

"The fags scare you?"

"No, I don't get scared, just you want to let them know they're not going to break the law, the law's going to break them. If they resist arrest on top of it, well, it can get a little rugged for them."

"Okay, Officer, thanks for the information. Tell Rodriguez hi for me," Marlon said. He handed the pad back then rolled up the window. The cop was dismissed.

"Keep making those movies, Mr. Brando, we'll all be watching." The cop walked back to his car.

Marlon knew that sooner or later they—whoever "they" happened to be—would discover he was Marlon Brando and

that would make his behavior, almost any behavior, accept-
able. But even without his celebrity Marlon would confront
authority believing that he was smarter, had higher octane fuel,
greater commitment. He could outact them and dominate.

The police car backed up, turned left, its headlights sweep-
ing through our interior, and drove away. We talked about
how heterosexual couples up and down the beach could be
fucking like stoats and all they'd get was a rebuke or a dirty
comment. Two fornicating males would be brought in and
worked on.

"Ever do fruity?" Marlon said.

"No. I have nothing against it, I just don't get the urge
about another guy. You?"

"No. Around the theater there are always guys hitting on
you, but I never got into anything," Marlon said. "There was
talk, they talked about Wally Cox and me."

"There's talk about you and me."

"Yeah, the assholes that write the gossip columns want it
to be true. The press says anything that sells newspapers, they
don't give a shit, they know you won't sue, it would just call
attention to the allegation. And if one out of fifty does sue,
they're insured. That's why I don't read any of it, I never
respond to it."

"So it's okay for us to kiss in public?"

"Sure, holding each other's butts."

We chuckled. Then just sat looking at the ocean.

"There was this girl who had been on several of the last
pictures I made," Marlon said, "loves to fuck, great fuck,
handles on her ass. We do it in the trailer, on the roof, my
house, her house. She's married. One night I was at her house,
I'm in the saddle, and her husband comes in the front door.

I'm pulling up my drawers and waddling to the window like a guy in a French farce hoping the husband doesn't want to fight. But he's real pleasant when he comes in, Señor Brando, happy to meet you, so good to have you in our house."

I laughed, not just at the perfection of the accent, but at the whole Mexican scene Marlon was creating. I'd always think when he started one of these improvisations that there should be an audience, this was his finest acting, it's too good for just one person to be seeing.

"I'm not sure how to take this *mi casa es su casa* shit, there's sex smells everywhere from me and his Rose of the Rancho, and that makes me a little tight with the smiling back. But he's frisky, he's rutting around and smiling and asking if I want anything—because he's not concerned about wifey, what he wants, you see, is to suck my cock. And my Spanish Rose is standing there with a smile saying yes, *sí, sí,* Marlon, is good."

"I hope you told him you didn't know him well enough."

"It was surreal, you can't just say thanks but no thanks. I just sort of whinnied and headed out."

"So you and Juanito going to make it a regular Friday-night thing?"

"It's not Juanito, it's . . . I don't even know what his name is."

"At Black-Foxe, my military school," I tell him, "there was this huge, fat kid. He always had sex books with pictures. He'd come into your room during study hours at night and let you read them. But he had to stay. You'd start looking at these naked girls and he'd put his hand on your dick. You'd whack it away. He'd put it back. You'd yank it off again and crack it hard. The whole thing would get faster and faster like a tinikling dance in the Philippines. And you'd look up and there was this puffed and purple face. That was a stopper. I'd close the book and give it to him. He would be shaking to have some kind of sex but he'd get up and go, he kept his dignity. It was kind of farcical and kind of tragic, in all that heat not one word was said between us."

"If you said anything to him it would mean you were sharing something with him," Marlon said as he looked out at the darkened ocean.

"Probably so."

"Amazing how mental sex is," Marlon said. "It's the idea that makes something sexually powerful."

"Yeah, the fantasies about what might be."

"And what mustn't be." Marlon responded. "I remember reading in Margaret Mead's book *Coming of Age in Samoa* about all their sexual taboos. You're not supposed to have sexual thoughts about your second cousin, so naturally all you can think about is throwing a leg over your second cousin. What kind of fantasies do you suppose that cop has?"

"Probably real mundane ones," I said. "Two badgers biting his balls."

"Yeah," Marlon added, "a zebra kissing him on the mouth."

"A little sexual frou-frou, Saran Wrap tied on his ears," from me.

Chuckling, quiet.

"It's crazy what people like you for," Marlon said. "They think that's you on the screen. That cop would like to be riding around on a motorcycle giving people shit the way I did in *The Wild One*. Ah, he's probably okay, but take away his flashlight and his nightstick and he's nobody."

"Yes. 'For what are kings when regiment is gone?' " I said.

"Shakespeare?" Marlon asked.

"Christopher Marlowe. *Edward II*."

"Who says it?" Marlon wanted to know.

"The king," I respond. "He's fled London, his army's gone, and only two of his retinue are left. He knows it's near the end. 'But what are kings when regiment is gone," he says, 'but perfect shadows in a sunshine day.' "

"How come you know a line from a Christopher Marlowe play?"

"I heard it, I thought it was beautiful, I wanted to remember it."

"But how come those things stick with you, George? Everybody wants to remember things, most people have trouble remembering their kids' birthdays."

"I don't get any credit, Mar, I didn't write it, I just remembered it."

"No, you don't get any credit, your brain is an anteater you don't have control of, it sniffs up information and whistles it into some filing box."

I laughed. "I think I remember things," I said, "because when I was a kid a lot of the time I didn't understand what was going on. If I remembered everything I'd be better prepared for whatever was coming next time."

"Yeah, fear is the best motivator. What was it again?"

" 'But what are kings when regiment is gone?' "

"Jesus, perfect," Marlon said.

For lunch, Marlon wanted to move into the living room. He got out of bed and we made the slow trek with the oxygen cylinder rolling behind us. As a matter of habit we sat opposite each other on the sofas in his living room, he at the far right end of his, I in the middle of mine. On the end table next to him is his phone with the many buttons on it. Punching them in different combinations he can talk to Angela wherever she is in the house. He can also, without being detected, monitor any phone conversation in the house. Everyone who works there knows this, so even the most trusted launder their conversations. Also on the end table is his CD player and two small speakers. He has stored a potpourri of selections from Nat King Cole favorites to Poulenc piano pieces. They play quietly in the background.

I am at peace, so many talks and meetings and parties and dinners have I been part of in this room. From my beginning days in the movie business, through meetings where directors were trying to lure Marlon into their projects, through unbearable moments after my son had died from drugs, and later, after Marlon's son killed his half sister's boyfriend, through all that happens in any forty-eight-year span, so much of it did we talk about here. This house, this room, are utterly familiar to me.

There is a fireplace on the wall to my left, his right, toward which the sofas are oriented, there is a wide, dark-wood coffee table between them. A vase, sometimes two, holds flowers that Angela has picked and arranged.

Marlon's two huge dogs are lying on the floor; Franny, a mastiff named for Marlon's sister, weighs, I would guess, over a hundred pounds, as does Sonny, a rottweiler. He is big and black with brown trim and a ballbearing-hard head. Angela has brought our lunch and set it on the coffee table. This is a cue for the dogs, they rise to participate. I am the guest, the target, I will offer least resistance, so they come to me, pushing in between the sofa and the coffee table. Franny comes first, Sonny tries to squeeze in beside her, but there isn't room, so he hangs back, his head above her withers.

Sonny has a little jocularity in him, he brings a playfulness to this food pursuit. Not Franny, the drool starts from under her dewlaps and she peers at me with mirthless eyes. "You and I are going to share what's on that plate," her expression says, "s'get some of it moving my way." She edges in closer, the black dewlaps and the dolorous eyes are over my thigh. She pushes her big head into my stomach. "That stuff on the table, s'go."

I take a piece of something off the plate and put it under her mouth. There is a spike in the room's sound level as her saliva-soaked mandibles pull apart and she hauls the morsel into her maw. You can put anything into that glopping machinery, items that are totally noncanine, olives with pits in them, asparagus, éclairs, escargots, all will be masticated then sucked down. The sopping sounds are punctuated by a snare drum rimshot as something hard is broken by her mandibles.

The sounds from Franny slow, then cease. Her spatula tongue tours her upper lip then goes back inside, her mouth is open. "That was good, ready for more." She shoves her head into my belly again. "S'go, champ, hook it up."

The immensity of her body, her head, her eating apparatus, her indifference to the texture or taste of what goes into her mouth, make me laugh. Franny doesn't share the fun, she pushes forward, dripping saliva on my pant leg. "Forget the giggling, more."

Marlon has watched the interlude intently, any behavior, animal or human, absorbs him. He coughs. He puts his right hand, made into a soft fist, in front of his mouth and rocks to prepare his body for the second cough that is coming. It arrives, a two-stroke bark. "Barrh-herm." He takes a deeper breath to prepare for the next wave of coughing. It's of Olympic quality, faster, higher, stronger.

"Ach, God." He coughs twice more. Nothing comes up, the pulmonary exertion has not improved his condition. He is wearing a cotton kimono, blue and white, loosely tied with an obi. The twisting and repositioning during the coughing have caused the kimono to open and I now have a good view of his belly and Jockey shorts.

"If I lean back it makes me cough," he says. But it seems to me the cough comes when it will, unrelated to how he is sitting. To avoid other coughs he has leaned forward, his elbows are resting on his thighs. Behind his arms the girdle of fat that surrounds his pectorals is visible; beneath that, outward and downward, flows his belly.

Because he's leaning forward he has to peer upward to see me, this brings wrinkles to his forehead. Facing me is an old man, nose and mouth pushed closer together, hair gray and straggly. The cough comes again; we wait it out. The spasm holds through three, four, five more coughs, neither of us can avoid noticing.

"Mar," I say, "with all the advances in medicine, isn't there a suppressant that would stop what's making you cough? You don't bring anything up, there doesn't seem to be an infection, so the cough seems to have no function, couldn't it just be suppressed?"

"There's scar tissue in the bottom of both lungs. They don't know what causes it. I have an idiopathic pulmonary syndrome, meaning there's something wrong but they don't know what it is." He paused. "It's what Franny died of."

"So it could be genetic."

"Probably is. But they know a lot more today than they did when she died. It'll get better. And if it doesn't, fuck it, I'm not afraid, it can come anytime."

He is leery of the people he has to talk to that he doesn't want to talk to, weary from the money he has to make to keep his world functioning. He isn't going to die right away, but now it is thinkable that one morning he might not wake up, or one day he might be seized with a coughing fit that he can't stop, he'd be on the floor like an upside-down insect trying to roll over and get his breath. And unable to.

2

It should frighten me; Marlon is eighty and I am seventy-seven, so death for either of us would be unsurprising. If he is on the trail to the end of his life, then so must I be winding toward my own. But my mind does not focus on that notion, I feel a restlessness, an impatience. In Tennyson's poem "Ulysses," the conqueror of Troy is an old man. He says to his fellow mariners, those who had fought and sailed with him:

> You and I are old;
> Old age hath yet his honor and his toil.
> Death closes all; but something ere the end,
> Some work of noble note, may yet be done, . . .
> . . . Come, my friends,
> 'Tis not too late to seek a newer world. . . .

I would like Marlon to be suffused as I am with this idea, I want to lift up his arms and clap his hands and say, "Let's dance, Mar." But where he is the music of exhilaration sounds only faintly. He is tired and we move back to the bedroom, he lies down and turns onto his left side, the position in which he believes the coughing doesn't come so often.

That night back in February I lay in bed thinking about Marlon and me and the long years we've known each other. It seemed to be nothing more than that, an idle reverie, then the thoughts quickened and images swelled and the entire zodiac of our experiences opened before me. The days, the era when Marlon stood astride the world. Our dinners with presidents and prime ministers, our double dates on every continent, Marlon dancing the hip-snapping tamure, every bit as expert at it as the Tahitians he's in the middle of. Music from a gamelan orchestra in Bali rises and recedes, then reggae from Jamaica, then the white voices of the Vatican Boys' Choir. The perfume that the wife of the prime minister of France wore when we sat on either side of her at the Paris opera; the thick, sick smell of coconut oil that hung everywhere in the Jakarta nights. I slid backward through this galaxy, back to our oldest memory, the night we met. In 1956.

Something impossible happened that year, two airliners—a United flight going east, a TWA flight going west—collided at thirty-three thousand feet over the Grand Canyon, killing 128 people. Elvis was singing "Love Me Tender," his big hit that year. The Soviet armies had invaded Hungary, Don Larsen had pitched a perfect game in the World Series, *My Fair Lady* had opened at the Majestic Theatre in New York. And, at a party in Los Angeles given by Burgess Meredith, Marlon and I were about to meet.

Two years before, a play called *Teahouse of the August Moon* had won the Pulitzer Prize. Marlon was going to play the lead role, Sakini, in the movie version, and Burgess was then performing the role in the road company in Los Angeles. Marlon knew Burgess and admired him, they were both patients of Dr. Bela Mittleman, a psychoanalyst in New York, so when Burgess suggested giving a *Teahouse* party for the two Sakinis, Marlon accepted. And that made the party an event.

Marlon was not *of* Hollywood, he dominated the industry but he didn't participate in the social scene. He was remote and disdainful of Hollywood studios and Hollywood money. So when word got out that he was coming to the party, anyone who could get an invitation—stars, producers, directors, studio heads—showed up.

Marlon had surged like a new celestial body into America's vision. First on the stage, then in film, he had revolutionized acting. He was sexual, violent, morose, unpredictable. He was boorish yet with an almost translucent sensitivity. He was noble, thoughtful, inexplicable.

The October 11, 1954, edition of *Time* magazine had Marlon, as Napoleon, on its cover. The story inside ran for six pages and was mostly a search for a way to describe him.

Six pictures in four years—*The Men, A Streetcar Named Desire, Viva Zapata!, Julius Caesar, The Wild One, On the Waterfront*—have branded the Brando name and face blue-hot on the public mind. The big studios, which are capable of taking endless pains to exploit either a valuable property or an eccentric personality, have not yet been able to answer the question, what is Brando?"

"Brando is just the best actor in the world," says Elia Kazan. "At moments he can vanish into the character he is portraying like a salamander under a stone or a tiger into the reeds."

"The only other place I've seen such a terrifying shift of identity is in a schizophrenic ward," said one playgoer.

Not only the *Time* article, but everything written about Marlon then asked the same questions: Who is he? What created that phenomenal acting ability and that outsider personality? The questions are still asked now.

I had toured with Burgess in two summer-stock productions, he had been a mentor to me, and I think he had an inkling Marlon and I would find common ground.

The house Burgess had rented was in West Hollywood, not a mansion but commodious and tastefully appointed. Marlon, in black leather jacket—everyone else wearing suits and ties—arrived late. There were two women with him, one on either side. Burgess and the three of them moved from the front door toward the living room, which was two steps down. That's where the rest of us were. They paused, and the great names of the movie industry stared at Marlon as normally they were stared at. The four descended and the crowd parted in a sort of Oriental obeisance to this enigmatic ruffian who was their regent. It was almost comical, these stars and moguls completely off stride, wondering if maybe they should curtsy or bow.

The two women were mysterious. They were alluring but discernibly not Hollywood. Celia was petite and dark-haired, her sexuality heightened by the look of efficiency she also wore. Reiko, Japanese, a Jack Cole dancer, attached only to Marlon, seeing only Marlon, moved with lissome grace.

Easy and confident as he followed Burgess through the introductions, Marlon had that smile that held you fifteen feet away even as you shook his hand. Flanked by the two seductive women, he was charismatic, semidivine. The other guests watched him with wide eyes, here he was in the flesh, what might he do?

Cloris Leachman, to whom I'd been married for five years at that time, had been at the Actors Studio with Marlon in its glory days in New York when it was run by Elia Kazan. I was staging nightclub acts in Las Vegas and directing a play I had optioned called *Please Communicate* at the Pasadena Playhouse; I was trying to get a foothold in the business.

Marlon detached himself from the rest of the party and came over to us. He kissed Cloris and introduced Celia and Reiko. Then he turned to me.

"Hi. Marlon Brando," he said.

"Glad to meet you, Marlon. George Englund."

Neither of us had an awareness at that moment that something important might be happening, there was no drumroll, no salvo of ordnance, no sustained note played on the shofar. With eighty other people around holding their drinks and cigarettes—smoking was in vogue then—it was just another social moment where you were nodding, smiling, saying hello. As you shook hands there was no hint of the life experiences you would explore with this fellow in front of you.

There was no foretelling of the significance that laughter would hold for you, of how almost religiously you would polish your talents to make each other laugh.

And nothing in that first exchange of salutations said that what would bind you most of all was fathers. You would learn that Marlon hated his father and he would learn that you didn't have one, so you would push toward each other and accept from each other the torrents of feelings you had about fathers. And, absent your real ones, you would do for each other what fathers do, you would counsel, encourage, and teach each other.

"I always wanted to see who Cloris would marry," Marlon said as he surveyed me, then he turned to Cloris.

"Well, Cloris—*Clorass*—what have you been doing?"

"Raising kids, Marlon."

"How many?"

"We have two boys."

"Going to have any more?"

"Ask George." She smiled.

"George, more children?"

"Not sure, Marlon, haven't figured out what's causing it." It was an old burlesque line; Marlon recognized it and laughed.

"Is George the reason you were late to the studio so many times?" He was speaking to Cloris but looking to me.

"Cloris didn't need my help, she's world-class at being late. Getting her to be on time is the problem."

"You and I won't live long enough." Marlon smiled.

We all smiled; it was true about Cloris, her irrepressibility was well known at the Studio. She smiled, too, enjoying the attention.

The other guests peered around one another's heads to figure out why Brando had selected that group to spend the evening with.

"I always thought Cloris was the most talented of all of us at the Studio," Marlon said. "One day we were doing improvisations—we were supposed to come to class in work clothes—and Kazan said get on the floor and choose to be a reptile. I was thinking about being a monitor lizard and I looked over—and there was Cloris in a pink suit on her belly."

"A Bergdorf Goodman suit," Cloris said. "But how was my improvisation?"

"Eerie. Pink suit, stockings, makeup, she made all that disappear, you believed you were actually watching an alligator," said Brando.

With that, Cloris dropped to the floor and began her alligator improvisation. Eerie *was* the word; her inventiveness was hypnotizing. Other conversations halted, all eyes were on Cloris on the floor reaching out with her reptile limbs.

As the party was breaking up, Marlon said, "You free tomorrow night?"

"I think so, sure."

"I've got a date with Anna Magnani." Magnani was the reigning Italian movie star, known for being earthy and lusty.

"She's going to try to fuck me," said Marlon, "I need some protection, can you and Cloris come?"

We agreed we could.

"We'll protect you, Marlon," I said.

After dinner at the Tail o' the Cock the next night we were driving through Beverly Hills in Marlon's Mercedes, Marlon and Magnani in front, Cloris and I in back. Magnani was like a middleweight getting a title shot. From the start she was closing on Marlon, pawing at him. It was clear she would have liked it a lot better if Cloris and I weren't there, which was, of course, why Marlon wanted us. Cloris and I sat upright like two Grant Wood figures.

Magnani's English was limited, she hammered out sentences without predicates and was impatient when we seemed not to grasp their meaning.

"Capisce o non capisce?" she barked at me. "You understand or you don't understand?" It carried a connotation of "How did America win World War II with guys with IQs like this one?"

"Marlon, why we don't go to your house, *caro*, we drop them to take a coffee somewhere." She was dying to get him alone.

"They're from out of town, I have to drive them home after I take you to the hotel."

"Where they live?"

"Fresno."

"What Fresno?"

"The intellectual capital of the world," I offered.

"They no have car?"

"Not after dark, George has a pigment problem in his eyes. Tell her about the ripples, George."

"It's not easy to talk about, but if I drive after dark I get these tiger stripes that come in waves; it would be easy to kill somebody."

"What kill? Come, Marlon." Her shoulder turn showed she was reaching for his crotch. "We take a ride to your house, I show you something."

Above everything in this life Marlon did not want to see what Anna had to show him.

"Marlon," I said, "you and Anna are so excited about each other, you kids ought to be alone." His eyes shot fire at me in the mirror. "Cloris and I'll jump a cab."

"You shit," he mouthed.

"Shucks, we remember feeling young and crazy like you and Anna. You don't want Ma and Pa Kettle in the backseat watching everything you lovers do, isn't that right, Anna?"

"Che adetto lui?" she asked Marlon. What did he say?

"He said he's fearful of what's going to happen to him tomorrow because he broke the American record for assholery tonight."

We had a rare time and we stayed with Marlon while he dropped Magnani at her hotel. In the days after that, often when I came home in the evening, Marlon would be there playing with our two boys or talking with Cloris, but he was waiting for me. He and I would get in the car and drive around for a while then go someplace for dinner. We'd sit talking and gesturing like Lenin and Trotsky plotting the revolution. But in the still waters underneath our joking lay that subject of such importance to both of us, fathers. Like archaeologists at a dig, slowly we uncovered the cities where our feelings about our fathers lay buried.

Constantly in his youth Marlon was fed his father's anger and alcoholism, forced to endure the man's absences and learn of his infidelities. When his father did come home, he was derisive, dismissive, and derogatory about his son's ability to do anything.

Mountainous anger seized up in Marlon and for the rest of his life he would lay a lick on anyone who even resembled a father or held a father's authority.

Marlon made vivid his childhood loneliness and isolation,

but as I listened I had a sense of excitement—how wonderful to have a father to have such powerful feelings about. And his father had given him his name, he was Marlon Brando Jr., his father had sent Marlon to Shattuck Military Academy, the school he'd gone to, which meant he wanted his son to be well educated. His father had done things that showed he cared.

"He didn't care," Marlon said, "he was an absentee landlord."

I never knew my father, Harold Austin Ripley. He was also an alcoholic, gone from our apartment in Washington, D.C., when I was six months old. I knew from my grandmother, a Jewish immigrant from Russia, a dear and lovely woman, that he was Catholic and a drinker. My grandmother, my sister, occasionally my mother, and more remotely my grandfather, were the principals in my earliest years. I did not understand why my father wasn't there and in the private part of my soul. I longed for him to come and balance the unwieldy mobile of life, to teach me to be proud of something, perhaps of myself. Throughout my life I searched for my father, I searched for him in Marlon. Marlon sought a better father in me.

When Marlon and I met, Cloris was pregnant with our third child and we lived in a small house on Beverly Glen Boulevard, a mile above Sunset Boulevard. Beverly Glen was a calm little thoroughfare then, not the congested artery between West Los Angeles and the San Fernando Valley it is now. On our black-and-white television set we watched Marlon win the Oscar for his performance in *On the Waterfront*. He was handsome in his dinner jacket and we applauded when he went up to receive his trophy.

Three days later Marlon was at the house when I came

home. I congratulated him on the award and we talked about it—not very much, he didn't have a great interest in it. Different from most of our freewheeling sessions, there was something specific he'd come to talk about.

"I mentioned a couple of times I was forming my own production company; remember?" he began.

"Sure."

"Well, they've poured holy water on it, made the sign of the cross over it, and now I'm a corporation. My mother's maiden name was Dorothy Pennebaker, so I've called it Pennebaker."

I offered my hand and we shook. "Good going, Marlon, big businessman now."

"I was thinking," he said, "it would be a good idea for you to direct the first picture."

That was a statement with nuclear power. Still, it was Marlon and me talking, I couldn't give the predictable reaction.

"Gee, that's really thoughtful, Mar, but my days are awfully full right now, I mean I have to be at unemployment at ten in the morning."

He laughed. "And you'll be working on your baseball-card collection in the afternoon, I can see it would be tough to fit this in."

"There you go. So maybe we could talk about it another time."

"I'll try you in a month, see if anything's loosened up."

Then we talked in earnest. It was so extraordinary a proposal it was hard to see it whole. A leap into the middle of the movie industry.

"It would be an honor, Marlon, more than that."

"I think it'll be good, I watch what you do, I listen when we talk, I think you can be a good director."

"Mar, this is exciting, but what occurs to me is the company hasn't produced a picture yet and I haven't directed one yet. Maybe I should be the producer first; then, when there's a picture ready to go, we can decide if I should direct it."

"Great, yeah, that's good, somebody has to organize everything. I want you to meet my father, he's president of the company, just to get to know you, he doesn't have any real decision to make. I'll set it up for tomorrow."

We met the next day at Marlon's house on Laurel Drive in Hollywood. Marlon introduced me to his father and the first thing that struck me about Marlon Brando Sr. was his air of distinction, his seeming urbanity. He was heavyset with a substantial paunch, he wore a close-trimmed mustache that reminded me of Esky the aging rascal in the old *Esquire* magazine. But I was looking for what was behind that appearance, for an aspect of Zeus, some telling trait that would explain Marlon's acting heritage.

It didn't take long to learn more about Senior. A half hour of conversation proved the aura of sophistication was an illusion. He'd been a salesman in the Midwest; he spoke in a hypnotic monotone and sometimes slightly slurred his speech. Here was the origin of Marlon's much-imitated mumble, he'd inherited it directly from his father. But in Marlon the speech pattern wasn't a handicap, it was a mesmerizing attribute.

Brando Senior was a plodding sort of fellow. The personality of his son, the nimble youth who probed and explored and soared and dared, was nowhere visible in the father.

Yet, as I compared the physiognomies, the bone structures and postures, the genetic stamp was unmistakable. Marlon was muscular and still in shape, but I could see how one day he could morph into his father's portly figure. Some other of Marlon's famous mannerisms, imitated by the thousands of actors who have wanted to be like him, were in the nods and head movements of his father. Yes, however far apart they might be psychologically, physically these men were indelibly father and son.

We talked about what sort of company Pennebaker could be. I said I thought we had an extraordinary opportunity to make excellent films and be profitable. I was ready to work hard to make the company successful. Senior mentioned that he was handling other investments for Marlon in cattle and oil. I was impressed, I had no idea how one managed those sort of investments. Later, it turned out he didn't either.

The talk was pleasant, we were getting to know each other, and I was hopeful that Brando Senior and I would get on well together. I can't say we did, there was always a distance between us. From the beginning I felt he didn't really like me, thought perhaps I wasn't terribly able, and I had grown up in Beverly Hills—that made him suspicious. But Senior didn't need a reason to be suspicious, by nature he was mistrustful of most things and nearly everybody. It didn't help that he had been thrust into a complicated industry with an arcane caste system.

Meetings with Brando Senior were not about making movies, they were occasions for him to convey his strong notion that you either had done, or soon would do, something truant. Further, and he'd accent this with an eyebrow elevation, when you did, he would promptly have knowledge of it. Senior passed this legacy to his son, who became the undisputed master of mistrust. Being suspicious was a cottage industry in Senior's hands; in Marlon's it became cosmology.

I've looked back to see what I might have done to create a happier relationship with Senior. I might have tried to understand him better, given more thought to the difficult position he was in, taken time to know his history. I could have tempered aspects of myself that I think worried him, been less exuberant, less at home in the corridors of Hollywood. I could have been a little more respectful.

But Senior didn't invite respect. It was hard to offer it because you felt you were intruding on the hard work he was doing to find the murky misdeeds that were undoubtedly going on in the Pennebaker tepee. I wanted to offer camaraderie, to say, "What is it, Senior, what fearful plot do you think is being concocted? Do you imagine that Bob Parrish, the director we were thinking of hiring, and Bob Dorff, my assistant, and I go out after work to scheme about how to gum things up at Pennebaker, how to jimmy another seventy cents out of our expense accounts? Say it, man, we'll face it together."

The frictions in my relationship with Senior were small compared to what went on between Marlon and him. That antagonism arched over everything. Appointing his father head of his company, like so much about Marlon, was a complex matter. Ostensibly he was sharing his success, giving his father a perch in the business world that the man had never enjoyed, or earned. But making Senior president of Pennebaker also provided a way to make war. Marlon could select a battle site and retaliate at will for abuses done to him in the long ago of his childhood. In a hundred subtle ways he could say to his father, "You were rotten to me when I was a kid, you didn't respect me, didn't love me, didn't believe in me. Now you're going to get paid back." And Senior took it, he was an ox who bore the yoke and the beating from his master.

One day the lava flowed. Marlon came into my office, ashen. He told me that his father had said he wanted to fire me. I don't remember Senior's reason, but I remember Marlon's fury, the tightness in his throat. His father had tapped into the boiling lake of Marlon's hatred of him. The patina of civility was gone. Marlon acted out how he had responded.

"Don't you ever say anything like that again," he had stormed. "This is my company, you hear me, you work for me and you don't hire or fire, you don't leave this fucking office unless I say so." With undiluted rage, with no tincture of remorse, he had taken his father's balls off, then cauterized him without an anesthetic.

Marlon Brando Sr. was Pennebaker's CEO, then, not because of his history as an executive, but by the sufferance of his son. His actions were under Marlon's surveillance, his decisions subject to Marlon's swift veto. Yet, to underline how complex human relations are, not infrequently when Marlon came to the studio he greeted his father with a hug.

There were times when a quiet madness prevailed at Pennebaker. Our first office was a small suite on the ground floor of a building on the Sunset Strip. It was unpretentious; in fact, it had no air-conditioning. One room was a pleasant reception area, the other was the office where I worked.

On an extremely hot afternoon in August, Marlon, his father, and I held our first company meeting at this office. I saw it as an important day and to prepare for it I had created a business plan that laid out Pennebaker's future. I'd worked hard on it, I wanted it to validate Marlon's confidence in me and show my bona fides as the chief operating officer of the company. I was alive with the possibilities I saw ahead.

Senior began the meeting. That was appropriate, he was head of the company, I figured he'd soon turn it over to me. But Senior had a bit more he wanted to say than I had imagined. It was disconcerting because from the beginning he talked in his languorous monotone, about a B flat below middle C. He discoursed on aspects of small-business operations; his talk might have had some relevance to little companies in the Midwest, but was unconnected to anything having to do with motion-picture production. The slow pace of his words and the brown monotone of his voice brought a heaviness to the room.

He'd asked at the beginning that I shut the windows to keep out the noise from Sunset Boulevard. I did and immediately the heat rose and magnified the closed-in feeling. By this point, some twenty minutes later, Senior's one-note drone had taken on a waffling effect.

He continued his treatise on small businesses. The lack of sequence, of relevance to our industry, our city, our world, our company, was total. He now began to insert elongated *ums* and *awms* between his phrases, all in that grating B flat. The room was getting hotter, Senior was perspiring, Marlon was perspiring, I was perspiring. I thought he might turn the meeting over to me now. He didn't; he talked on in that low reverb.

I started to feel just that tiny bit giddy, I needed Senior to talk for a second in a tenor voice, a falsetto even, a sopranic trill, anything to vary that relentless monotone.

No. "Subchapter S, awm, SBA loan, tax code section R, deduct travel, upward trend . . ."

A tongue of panic licked my insides, a drowsiness was coming on, my extremities were numbing. I put an arm across the back of the chair next to me and grinned to reassure Senior and myself, heigh-ho, doing fine, all good here, carry on. It didn't register on Senior, he was Frankenstein plodding through the forest, and his adenoidal boom was penetrating the bone that enclosed my head. I wanted to pull my lips back like an orangutan, I wanted to do physical harm to something. My business plan was becoming a gelatinous mass in my mind.

I fixed on Senior's Adam's apple; it hardly moved in the production of the drone. Nothing moved, his mandibles seemed not to move. He began to shimmer in front of me, a seductive swami stealing my brain. "You're going to sleep," said the voice inside my head. "Don't care," came the response from my softened cortex. His voice was funereal now, awm oom, awm oom, it was impossible to struggle, I was in thrall to him.

"We awm wouldn't list assets until oom awm second year um accountant in Omaha Harold very knowledgeable . . ."

My mouth was open like a crocodile's. "ZZZZZ!" I heard it come out of me, it frightened me.

"Tax shelters, write-downs, onetime annualize, capitalize, carmelize awhm, oohm, oooohm."

Wondering how Marlon was surviving, I turned a dry eyeball to him, he was awake, he looked like he was listening, God, this was too freaky. I didn't want to fall sleep, I wanted to be a success for my children, for my school. "ZZZZZZZ!" My head banged forward, my neck cracked.

I pulled up with a starlet smile. Was it believable? Who cares, it's so hot and boring I can't see. I need saliva, I need oxygen, I need a gun.

"Double ledger quarterly assumable industry norms cash reports accounting same as drop forge and tool ledgering . . ."

From the crab nebula Senior's words descended to my hearing apparatus, which was now made of farfalle.

"George, where do you think we'll be in our output in six months?"

He had stopped. There was silence. I kept my eyes closed to look as if I were framing an answer. Easy, I thought, try a few words, don't go for whole sentences. I started to talk, it came out adenoidal and Chinesey, but hearing my own voice was reassuring. I eased into second gear, gathering words into sentences, carefully I segued to the subject of literary acquisitions, how making the right choices would assure quality in our films.

I was up in the saddle now, talking with confidence, I introduced the subject of Pennebaker tying up with a major production/distribution company, which would take care of our overhead and give us not only a business home but better access to material. All right! I was happening, I was a young executive with vision and high goals, I was leading the way to—

Suddenly the sound of a million buzzing mosquitoes filled the room, what could it have been? Marlon and I turned to each other. Then our eyes went to Senior.

He was out cold. Poleaxed, *X*'s over his eyes. His hands were across his belly, his chin nailed to his chest, the clatter coming out of his uvula was shaking the room.

Marlon was thrilled; in front of him established order was

descending into anarchy. He watched his father, entranced, then he turned to me and gave me a thumbs-up.

"Georgie, I saw your talent early, but you've broken out of the pack, you may be the greatest bore in the history of the film industry."

He was right. With only my visions of the company's future and what I thought were a few colorful illustrations—with only that meager equipment I had put this buffalo away in under four minutes.

"Dad!" Marlon hollered. His father's head came up and his eyes looked to the window. "No, here. You fell asleep."

Senior turned and peered at us, not sure who we were. It was a supremely awkward moment. He had definitely gone to sleep, so should he apologize? Yes, certainly. But hold on, he was head of the company, maybe George should apologize for having driven him into that stupor.

Questions arose in my mind. What about the future, would our next meeting go this way? Would there be a next meeting? If there was, should Senior drop some speed before we started? Should I find another line of work?

The questions were moot because the company took a big step forward. We made a deal with Paramount Pictures to produce three films. In 1956 we moved to the Paramount lot on Melrose Avenue, to the second floor of the Executive Office Building.

The decision at Pennebaker was that our first picture should be a western. Marlon as a western hero seemed a strong commercial idea.

An agent named Maury Grashin brought in a manuscript called *To Tame a Land,* the newest novel by his author Louis L'Amour. It had interesting characters and good western perfume, but the narrative wandered a bit and sometimes lost tension.

This was just before L'Amour became a favorite author of several of our recent presidents and found a wide reading public. His novels, now in paperback, still fill the shelves at airport bookstores.

We met at L'Amour's apartment in the Garden of Allah on Sunset Boulevard. From the first there seemed something askew, Louis L'Amour didn't look like a western writer, he wasn't wearing a lanyard or frontier pants or boots. He was a large man with wavy black hair that suggested a Greek Mafia don whose boats ran hashish out of North Africa. He had some sort of handicap, his movements were extremely limited, he never got up from the table while we were there. I didn't find out what the handicap was.

All the table surfaces in his living room were covered with books, articles, and manuscripts on the West; he quoted incidents and supplied colorful anecdotes in an old storyteller's way. I found him compelling but also felt there was some sort of con going on. He gave us new facts about Wyatt Earp and the gunfight at the OK Corral—that Wyatt pronounced his name *Arp*, not *Urp*. He was supplying all this new information on one of the best-known moments in Western history. Where did he get it, how come nobody knew it before?

You wanted him to connect the dots, bridge the chasms of inconsistency, but before you could tap him on the arm, he was on to the next piece of lore. If you really pushed your nose in, he'd fix his black eyes on you more penetratingly and give you some more sundae toppings.

"I was the only white man who has ever been at an inner council tribal meeting of the Apache, the only place where these stories are told. That other part you're asking about—that came direct from Frank James's two grandnephews, who told it to me one sweltering, drunk night in Wyoming."

His minitales might not have been connected, but each one glowed in his telling. He put his own paprika on them, and Marlon, particularly, was fascinated. The details and the hardware that L'Amour talked about so gloriously were exactly the kind of thing Marlon loved.

I wasn't sure there was a whole story in the book, but owning a novel meant we had the beginning of our first film. That might have made *To Tame a Land* seem to be a more complete tale than it was. We optioned the book.

We announced in the trade papers that Pennebaker had acquired *To Tame a Land* as the first vehicle for Marlon Brando in his own company. Literary agents crowded through the door suggesting screenwriters. Bob Dorff and I talked with literary agents, read scripts, interviewed writers, and pared them down to a short list. It was time to discuss the candidates with Marlon.

"Let's not meet at the studio, come up to the house," Marlon suggested.

"Okay, see you in the morning at ten."

"I'll probably be downstairs playing the congas."

His old hillside home on Laurel View Drive had three levels, the lowest being one very long room with a high ceiling and a polished wood floor. Except for Marlon's equipment at the far end, it was empty. In front of two huge speakers were Marlon's three conga drums.

Afro-Cuban music cranked to a deafening level, insistent, repetitive, was booming out of the speakers and off the wood floor. Marlon sat in front of the speakers facing three-quarters away from me, dripping in music and sweat. His playing was so abandoned, his immersion so total, it seemed no one should be watching, he wouldn't release himself this way if he knew anyone was in the room.

I stood observing him and it started to seem awkward. If he turned around and saw me standing there, it could scare him, it could even seem suspicious, why hadn't I said I was there when I entered? On the other hand, if I suddenly yelled out, "Hey, Mar, want to go to work?" it could frighten him even more.

I walked toward him with a smile so if he did turn around he'd see friendly. He didn't look up, just kept firing on the drums. Well, he knew I was coming, he couldn't be too startled, I should just go up and announce myself. Still I felt uneasy because vocally I'd have to come in over the level of the music. I went up to about six feet from him. *"Hey, Mar,"* I bellowed.

Mistake. He leaped out of the chair as if four hundred volts had gone through his body. His leg shot out and kicked the drum he was playing and it skidded across the floor on its side and banged against the wall. His eyes were staring, atavistic. The Niagara of sound made it difficult to note casually that I was here to talk about writers.

"Jesus, you shouldn't—scared the living shit out of me." I read his lips.

I used Italian arm waves. "I was trying not to, I was trying to look normal."

He stalked around, directionless, then went to the stereo and shut it off. The sudden cessation of noise was unearthly.

"Give somebody a heart attack, get somebody killed," he said too loudly, forgetting the sound was no longer there.

"Next time let's meet in the kitchen, I'll honk first then ring the doorbell."

He smiled a tight one, but his mind was still with the Yoruba Top 40. Sweat covered his forehead, his T-shirt was soaked through, I was wearing a suit and tie, we seemed to have nothing in common.

"Want to talk about writers?" I said.

"Shit no, writers is the last thing I want to talk about. Let's go upstairs."

That memory of Marlon playing his congas is vivid to me now. More than a picture of a man playing drums, it's the essential marrow of Marlon. He was alone, his head was cocked to the blast of the beat, his hands flew as the African voices chanted and the cowbells punctuated. He wanted to be as primitive as they, as free of custom, as fused with rhythm and feeling. His shoulders worked, his fingers popped the skins, he recoiled, attacked, stronger, faster, down the long tunnel of passion and violence he went.

Upstairs we talked about everything except writers. In the kitchen Marlon put together some breakfast items. He is careful when he cuts an orange, precise when he butters the toast, he makes his *petit déjeuner* look appealing. We sat in the breakfast room.

"Your motor's running, Georgie," he said

"It is, Marlon."

"Young man on the way to his rendezvous with destiny?"

"I'll wait on the rendezvous, settle for picking a writer today."

"We will."

"Ready to go over the list?"

"Shit no, I only said we'd do it, I didn't say when." He smiled. "Okay, now."

I brought out the list. "Stanley Groves, remember him?"

"Yeah, we met him at Arthur Loew's party the other night."

"Right."

"Dorky guy, funny looking, walks funny. What's wrong with him?"

"I'm not sure, I didn't want to bustle up and say why are you dipping and rising that way."

"Be interesting to know, though. Did you talk to his wife?"

"Daphne, yeah, beautiful, I'd met her before."

"I spent a long time talking to her," Marlon said. "What an odd marriage, what's in it for her?"

"There's always the possibility she loves him."

"The odd forms love takes. I suppose she does love him, that's the only thing that would explain why she takes that kind of care of him. Anyway, I fucked her after the party. Next day she came up to the house for lunch. I think she does love him."

"That's my impression, she seems very loyal to him."

"I guess so, but it's a little hard to fit fucking me into that loyalty program."

"You're Marlon Brando, legend, night rider, you shine your light on somebody, she's vulnerable. The sad thing is she's not fucking you, she's fucking the image."

"That's what I hate. In this town fucking is a technique you develop, like dentistry. You get good at it, you're going to do a lot of fillings."

"I sort of doubt Daphne will come up to the house again," I said.

"No, I don't think so either."

"Maybe you'll be a good boy and not suggest it."

"I don't plan to . . . there is something sad about it."

"Okay, good, Mar, in under two hours we've covered Stanley Grove's domestic life and whether you should fuck his wife again. Want a look at his screen credits or is that irrelevant?"

Three hours later we did make a choice, Niven Busch, who had a good list of western credits.

The sense that there wasn't a developed story in our book deepened because Busch's screenplay didn't work. After him came Robert Buckner. He failed as well. The joke started around the office: *To Tame a Land* is one thing, to get a screenplay out of it is impossible.

But we didn't stop, and with Bob Parrish we were getting close to a good, promising structure. Marlon came to one of our story conferences with the look of a man newly baptized. He sat down to share his new vision.

"I'm not going to kill anyone in this picture," he said.

This was my first contact with Marlon's way of defoliating projects in mid-development. I thought the best thing to do was try to follow his thinking. He had a point, it wasn't good to make pictures about people killing people, everyone could agree with that. And there lies the rub. Marlon will make a point that is generally valid about life but, which if introduced into the project on which you are working, will distort or destroy it. It isn't that he doesn't make sense, it's that the sense belongs in a different context. As you try to pull his new idea into the story mass you get a glimpse of yourself in the padded room at Bellevue.

Marlon knew what a western was, we all did, that's why we wanted to make one. The story we bought, the story he liked, was about a man who made his living as a gunfighter.

He would survive to the end of the film because he won his gunfights; ergo, he would be killing people.

Since none of us knew what to say, there was a silence. Marlon fondled the phrase again: "I'm not going to kill anyone in this picture."

It was like being in a Zen class. The master says, "Today I give you two koans to dwell on. First, what is the sound of one hand clapping? Second, how do you make a film about a gunfighter who doesn't kill anybody? Think on it, my followers, in the way of Zen there is an answer."

Y. Frank Freeman, a Georgian who owned a large theater chain in the South, had become head of Paramount Pictures. It was to Mr. Freeman I reported each month on the progress of our projects. How would I carry Marlon's revised thinking on the next visit? "Afternoon, Mr. Freeman . . . yes, sir, I do have some news on our western, Marlon's come up with a hummer of an idea, he wants to give the picture a spiritual twist. What's a spiritual twist? No, ha-ha, no angels floating around, Mr. Freeman. Marlon sees the story going like this. He's had all human feeling squeezed out of him because of what's been done to his sister. He's finally cornered the guy that did it, the most hateful creature in the West. They're about to draw down on each other and you know human insides will be flying against the back bar any second. Now right here, Mr. Freeman, is where your spiritual twist comes in. Spiritual people don't kill anybody—so Marlon doesn't give you one of those pat endings where he pumps lead into this foul monster. No, sir. With the audience on the edge of its seats, Marlon goes over to this bad guy and starts to talk with him about his childhood . . . well, hold on, Mr. Freeman, I didn't think you'd get that upset, I can understand your thinking it doesn't sound like money, but let me just tell you that Marlon is certain we'll capture that entire pacifist audience out there."

Other thoughts were born. If Marlon was operating on this moral plane not previously revealed, how would it affect the whole agenda at Pennebaker? Would there be a Pennebaker? In the Brando ashram there were not a lot of clues.

3

B ack in the 1960s if your offices were at Paramount there were three main places to have lunch—Oblath's coffee shop across the street, Lucy's on Melrose, and the studio commissary. We usually chose the commissary, it was animated, all the filmmaking principals were there.

During one noontime a young actress named Anna Kashfi was lunching with her costars from *The Mountain,* Spencer Tracy and Robert Wagner. She was a revelation out of Marlon's dream book, brown skin, lustrous eyes, fatal smile, and over the commissary commotion, tinkling fragments of her English-Hindi accent. Anna was nineteen and beautiful and she had Marlon staring.

We got the publicity man to bring Marlon to the table and introduce him. In those moments Marlon is a lightfoot lad and gives some of his most charming performances. Struck by Anna, he turned it on, a little urbanity, a little shy guy, a

touch of European inflection, a soupçon of British good manners, no vulgarity, no Wild One. He delighted Anna and
entertained the table. Even the old man of the movies,
Spencer Tracy, had open admiration on his face. Marlon said
he would call Anna later. He didn't ask for her number, that
would be easy to find. The ancient Noh play was about to be
performed again.

Marlon asked me to go with him on his first date with
Anna. He was nervous, he was dressed handsomely in a suit
and chatted about Anna's attractions as we drove to her
apartment. He parked in front of her building and I waited at
the car, a two-seater Thunderbird. When Marlon reappeared,
Anna was on his arm, exquisite in a silk dress.

"You remember George."

"Yes, of course." She smiled.

Anna was happy but facing a problem—how were the
three of us going to get into that car, which was barely big
enough for two?

I opened the door for her. She peered into the interior.

"How do you think we should do this?" she asked with the
smile, the lilting English.

As Marlon and I poked our heads in, it was hard to see
how we could all fit. Another thought hovered; she was Marlon's date, and however we solved the seating problem, she
was going to be very close to me.

"We can do it," Marlon said. "Why doesn't she just
back in?"

"She backs in she'll come up against a gearshift real sudden, Mar, wouldn't want to see her do a lot of backing."

"It really is awkward and there are George's long legs to fit
in, too." Anna laughed.

One possible solution was for her to straddle the little island between the seats and ride it like a horse, but her dress would be up over her thighs and that was such a lurid picture that we all backed off from it.

Anna finally pushed in and got her left cheek onto the console and was facing me. I squeezed in, slammed the door, and Marlon took off. Within a few blocks the contortion was too much and Anna did the only conceivable thing. She slid onto my lap.

Marlon was looking forward, speaking about lilacs in bloom, telling Anna of his relish for life. He wanted to make clear his thoughts were on the spirit of man, not on anything as tasteless as getting into her knickers on the first date. He was selling it beautifully, but right beside him was I, laden with his trophy, Anna's svelte behind on my lap. More uncanny, the tight conditions left my hand nowhere to dwell but directly under her tits.

Marlon turned to play a dashing line to Anna and the configuration of bodies zoomed to his eyes: his new love and I were pressed together at a number of crucial places. I was clearly innocent, but nevertheless the sight was unsettling. From behind Anna I gave him a smile that said, "You know I wouldn't do anything crazy, Mar."

He looked to the road then back to me. With only eyebrow raises and fleeting smiles, my message was, "Mar, if I could tell you about the texture of this girl's ass, and—fasten seat belts for this one—when she leaned over to prop herself up, did she ever dump a blouse full of goodies on me. I'm your buddy, Mar, nothing to worry about there, but I got to tell you I'm sweating, big guy."

Marlon got the message and laughed. Then got back into

his story. He was keeping it animated, but it couldn't compare with the drama going on beside him.

When he looked over again I said, "Anna, are you comfortable?" I patted her knee and rolled my eyes to him.

"Yes, this is much better. Will we be at the restaurant soon?"

Not soon enough for Marlon, he mashed on the accelerator.

During dinner I watched the romance begin. Marlon and Anna were happy, they were beautiful and so pleased to be with each other.

I left before dessert and took a cab home; it was time for them to be alone, and that trip in the Thunderbird wouldn't have worked a second time.

Christian Brando is the only child of Marlon and Anna. At his hearing in the 1990s for the killing of Dag Drollet, his half-sister's boyfriend, the testimony about how he'd been raised was sad, the stories about his mother particularly disturbing. She'd apparently had Christian kidnapped and taken to Mexico, where he'd been found in the company of hippies who said they'd been hired by her. A friend recalled finding Anna lying in her apartment in her own vomit while outside baby Christian was playing unattended at the side of the swimming pool.

Anna seems to have lived a truly sorrowful life. Still, the memory of that young beauty at lunch in the commissary persists, as does that funny and romance-filled first date when each of them wanted so badly to seem right to the other.

I've wondered what life Anna might have had if she'd never met Marlon, never married him. How much did Marlon's way of treating women, the ancient score he always had to settle through them, affect her? If she hadn't been in the commissary that day, would she be an ordinary woman now with an ordinary—and drug-free—life? The question lingers because one thing I have seen to be indisputably so: if you're in love with Marlon, you're in rough company.

At Pennebaker some clouds were looming. Movie stars having their own production companies gave them ownership of their films, which in turn gave them more money and a better tax situation.

Marlon had no interest in corporate matters. And he had no urge to persevere through the arduous process of developing films. So when he received offers from other studios where all he had to do was act, he took them.

When Warner Brothers announced that Marlon was going to do *Savonara* for them, Mr. Freeman called me in. When was Paramount going to get its Brando picture? he wanted to know. Paramount was paying our overhead, our writers, and our research, and within a reasonable time they should get their picture.

"Paramount will make any film you fellows want to make. Give me anything but the phone book and we'll do it. And if it's the Atlanta phone book, I'm not sure we wouldn't make that with Brando. Englund, give me a date when you'll start a picture for Paramount."

I suggested to the Marlons that we find a completed script with a good plot and a strong role for Marlon. With it as a backup, we could give Paramount a firm production date. If none of our other projects was ready, we'd do the backup film. Everyone agreed to the plan.

We had a stroke of luck in our search for that backup: Bob Dorff found a western screenplay called _Yellow Leg_. It was professionally done, you could see the movie, and you could see Marlon in it. With a little work it would be just what we needed. In fact, it seemed good enough to most of us that we should certify it now as our first picture. When Marlon read it, he approved it and agreed that if we didn't have another script ready by September 15, 1958, we'd shoot this one. Bob Dorff and I began to polish the script of _Yellow Leg_.

I had also suggested another project to Marlon, a picture on the United Nations Technical Assistance Program. Dry-sounding words but potentially rich material for a film. It also fit with Marlon's wish to do a picture that would have a positive effect in the world.

Experts from the United States and other developed countries would agree to give two years to help people in a corner of the world they might never have heard of.

Some who went were young, some were retired, some brought their families, some fell in love and got married. Some died. In this mélange of human stories there was a good one for Marlon. He and I presented the idea to Mr. Freeman, who was inclined to like what Brando liked. Mr. Freeman said we should do it, Paramount would finance the research trip.

Marlon and I talked to Stewart Stern, who had just written _Rebel Without a Cause_. Stewart had great enthusiasm for the idea, and he became our writer. The three of us went to United Nations headquarters in New York to do our research and prepare for the journey that would take us through all of Southeast Asia.

That Marlon Brando and his company were planning a film about UN activities was strong news and the UN headquarters staff welcomed us. On our second day in New York, an unusual interlude started. Marlon, Stewart, and I went to lunch in the Delegates Dining Room. A positively smashing young lady was seated five tables away from ours. I laughed to myself, she was the Brando woman idealized. Indian, Junoesque, large eyes, a perfect mouth, animated and glowing. Her silk sari clung rather than concealed. She was so striking we thought she had to be a movie star.

Maxwell Dunn, who was from Australia and was our liaison with the UN, said she was an expert with UNICEF in child development. A graduate of the London School of Economics, she had gained a notable reputation in her field. Marlon asked if he could meet her.

We were in delicate country. Marlon wanting to meet the beautiful expert could appear as Hollywood vulgarity. In fact, the story that Stewart had begun to sketch out did have a Eurasian leading lady, and if this creature could act, and maybe if she couldn't, she'd be a candidate. There was an unmistakable resemblance to the meeting with Anna in the Paramount commissary.

Dunn received no sign of welcome as he approached the lady's table, her posture suggested that this unbidden arrival was an impropriety. She looked loosely in the direction of our table when Maxwell indicated Marlon, but her eyes were devoid of interest and the chill expression remained.

Dunn returned not with the usual "Oh, she'd love to meet you." Miss Jill Ranasingh was not clear why this group of movie people wanted to speak with her. If there was a legitimate issue, why hadn't it been presented through channels? However, she had agreed to reserve fifteen minutes at three o'clock.

Her office was not large and the four of us filled it up. Miss Ranasingh sat elegantly upright, she nodded as Maxwell gave our names and described our positions. Close up she was even lovelier, why wasn't she on the cover of *Vogue* every month?

"Yes, how do you do," she said in English minted with Hindi. She gestured toward the chairs. "Please sit."

I usually did the description of our project, but today Marlon told it. He did it well and through it Miss Ranasingh nodded in brief punctuation. When Marlon paused, she said, "Well, yes, I can see there might be an excellent film in the program, good luck with it." Her eyes moved from one to the other of us as if to say, "I'm not certain why you wanted to tell me about it."

It seemed so dumb, we were talking to her because Marlon had eyes for her; everybody in the room knew it. Why didn't we just say it? Marlon wound up reaching for the old Hollywood casting chestnut. There was a role in the script that she could be, er, would she be interested in reading the script when it was finished, incidentally, had she ever acted? He was interested in getting her into a conversation, but she was not interested in playing the flattered young beauty.

"No, I have never acted," she said pleasantly. A beat. "Was there something else?"

The situation was disintegrating, Marlon was getting nowhere, and we could be doing injury to our image as serious filmmakers. I tried to help. I said we already had a clear picture of how complicated an organization the UN is. But for us the issue was human stories, films are drama, they have to be about people, the audience has to be involved in the hopes and despairs of the leading characters. We had to learn those personal stories—hers, for instance. Was it possible she'd have a moment at the end of the day for a drink in the Delegates Lounge?

"Thank you, but I leave promptly at five-thirty today. Anyway, I'm afraid my department would have little to contribute, we are concentrating only on the problems of children. But if a question comes up, you can talk with Mr. Dunn, I'm sure he'll find the right people."

She rose and offered her hand. We all shook it. And we left. Class dismissed.

"Understand, she comes from a different tradition," Maxwell said. "It doesn't invite informality, that's just not how they behave in her caste."

But Marlon was not used to what amounted to rejection from a woman. He was frustrated and fractious two days later when he had to go back to California and had made no progress with Miss Jill Ranasingh.

Stewart and I remained in Manhattan, where we studied documentaries and reports from the field and I began setting up the itinerary for our research in Southeast Asia.

I walked into the Delegates Lounge to meet Stewart one evening and on the banquette, sitting by herself, was Miss Ranasingh. She waved, beckoning me over. When I arrived at her table she offered her hand.

"How are you, Mr. Englund?"

"Very well, thanks, and you, Miss Ranasingh?"

"Very well, too. Everything coming along nicely? Can you sit for a moment?" I sat in the chair opposite her. "I'm meeting some colleagues, but tell me quickly how your project is going."

"The truth is you never know how a film is going till you're sitting at the first preview, but we're paying attention and putting in the hours."

"Yes? Maxwell Dunn giving you everything you need?"

"He's been very helpful, we're lucky to have him."

"Good. Well, let us know if we can help, too."

Let us know if we can help, too—that was unexpected, and said so earnestly.

"Thanks, I'll do that, Miss Ranasingh."

"Jill. Why don't you call me Jill."

I paused. This was getting downright folksy. "All right, Jill."

"And I'll call you George if that's permissible."

"It is, it's what my mother calls me."

"I'll be in good company, then. Nice to see you this evening, George."

"Lovely to see you, Jill."

She still had the Brahman formality, but her attitude was discernibly different. One thing wasn't different, she was still just as gorgeous.

When I gave Marlon a progress report by phone that evening, I told him how differently she'd behaved.

"Maybe she's sorry she was so goddamn hostile," he said.

"Nothing about her says sorry, Mar, she's very self-possessed."

"Still look as good?"

"Every bit."

When I got back to Los Angeles to pick up Marlon and start on the trip to Southeast Asia, he asked if I'd seen Jill Ranasingh again. I had. Having never been rebuffed that way before, he wanted to know the aftermath. I told him.

The next time I saw Miss Ranasingh was also in the Delegates Lounge and she waved me over.

"How's it going, I haven't heard from you," she said.

"We've been caught up in our research and there are tons of things to get done before we leave. Stewart and I are at it all day every day."

"And all night every night? You are dedicated men," she said with amusement.

She was unmistakably different from the way she'd been when we first met her.

"Jill," I said, "could we go back to the day we met?"

"If you want."

"I'd like to get it in focus. It was clear to me, clear to all of us, that we were an intrusion and you were anxious for us to leave."

"Of course."

"Why was that?"

"Surely you know."

"I don't think I do."

"Mr. Brando was boorish to behave as if no one knew of his penchant for dark-skinned women, as if everyone in the dining room couldn't see the whole immature drama of his noticing me then arranging to meet me. Yes, I was anxious for that to end."

"It was poor, I can see we acted as if UN people are only interested in bringing food to Rwanda and have no interest in social things."

"UN people are interested in sex and money like everyone else. After that they're interested in bringing food to Rwanda."

"You weren't impressed at meeting Marlon Brando?"

"Oh, very impressed, my word, he's an exceptional actor, I adore to watch him."

"Why couldn't a little of that have shown?"

"I wouldn't have wanted him to know that . . . though he is madly rakish. What I did want both of you to know is that I think you have a wonderful project. Getting through the UN bureaucracy will be very challenging, but I hope you will stay with it and produce your film."

It was a spur. Stewart and I finished our work with renewed vitality. Of equal importance, I told Marlon I felt that if he was patient, and courtly, improbable as it had seemed at first, the door to Miss Ranasingh's bedroom might be ajar.

But alas, Marlon never found his way there. This might have been the first, and last, rebuff for the legendary lothario.

4

—

It was April 1958. We'd taken all our inoculations, packed our tropical clothes and our UN credentials. We held a press conference the day before we left, then we were off to dent the world. We were unaware that, as with so many movies, our UN project would follow a marathon course. What we learned on this trip would eventually be used in the making of *The Ugly American*. Herman Leonard, a photographer from New York, was with us to record Marlon's journey of research.

In the airport lounge at LAX, waiting to board, we were an excited little band, we'd take off to the west over the Pacific, and when we returned we'd be flying in from the east, having circled the world.

Just before we boarded I was given a bill for $1,200 for overweight. It was a shock, I had no idea what it was for. The next morning in Honolulu I said we'd better see what every-

body was taking, we couldn't haul that kind of weight through the rain forests. Marlon was as curious as I.

We lined our bags up in our living room and the problem lay spread before us. Neatly spaced and side by side were Marlon's barbells, four hundred pounds of iron. He had also brought two tall conga drums in their cases. We made fun of it, we improvised carrying his weights to a meeting with a village headman on the slope of a volcano. Beginning of the voyage humor. We sent the weights and drums back to the studio.

Honolulu, Guam, Wake, finally Manila. We flew on a Boeing Stratocruiser, maybe the most comfortable airplane for passengers ever built. And absolutely one of the slowest. It cruised at 285 miles per hour; the trip was endless. On the last leg to Manila, while the rest of us were sleeping, Marlon was watching oil collect on the cowling of the inboard port engine. He worried and surveyed, keeping to himself the dread knowledge that the engine was about to ignite. He finally hailed the flight engineer, who said the oil was normal in these engines, everything was performing perfectly. It was too late to salvage the nervous energy and lost hours of sleep. With his puffed eyes Marlon looked Oriental himself as we let down to Manila.

I was worried that the Paramount representative hadn't been advised we were coming and we might not be met at the airport. The concern evaporated when I looked out the window; you couldn't see the tarmac for the white shirts. The city of Manila seemed to be at the airport to greet Marlon Brando.

We came out the door and our eyes went to slits, the tropical sun was blinding. The crowd surged past the police and at the bottom of the stairs we were sucked into a roiling mob. We took a pounding and all of us lost parts of our clothes, but we got to the cars. The frightened limousine drivers honked, stopped and started through the hysteria.

We were time-lagged and tense. Marlon dislikes crowds and always avoids them and this one was amok. He was drawn. I shared his alarm; if a mass this size turned violent, there would be no way to get out of it, something catastrophic would happen.

Herky jerky, stop and go, with faces plastered up against our windows, we managed to get out of the airport and onto the road to Manila. Motorcycle riders, sometimes four on one bike, swung in and out to get next to our car. Every kind of vehicle jammed up close, the people screaming, peering in, unconcerned that our whole lunatic flotilla was rolling toward town at sixty miles an hour.

Marlon, Stewart, and I started the next morning on our research meetings with the doctors, scientists, and agriculturists of the UN. The first three days were wall-to-wall meetings.

After lunch on the fourth day we needed time to breathe, to assess where we were and what we'd seen. We wanted to hear the sounds and see the colors of the Philippines, but we couldn't leave the Manila hotel without a police escort. If Marlon got out in the open he'd be surrounded. He and I had the same bursting feeling to get out and have some excitement.

The Manila hotel is built in a quadrangle that encloses a large central lawn. Marlon and I surveyed it and the thought came that it would be a good place for a game of touch football. Marlon had brought a football, too.

Stewart Stern is a writer, sensitive, artistic, as fine a man and talent as you will meet, today still one of my dearest friends. With no athletic background. Herman Leonard, our photographer, a slim man from New York, also had limited athletic experience. It was decided Stewart and I would play Marlon and Herman.

We kicked off. Marlon caught the ball and started upfield. As I went for him he threw me a head-and-shoulders fake that I bit on. I checked, whipped around, and chased him across the field. I tagged him, going flat out. He sidestepped between the hibiscus bushes, I had too much velocity, I shot through the hibiscus hedge and crunched into the wall of the hotel. Marlon slipped then crashed, too. It was a shaker bouncing off the wall at that speed, but neither of us bothered with the effect. Almost immediately we were in a ferocious competition. We trotted back to the field.

As Marlon and Herman huddled, I talked defense with Stewart. He listened but was distracted, he later said, by the absence of any sense that we were playing a game. He and Herman both noticed the fury with which Marlon and I chased and blocked each other.

But our mania was contagious and the two library types were drawn in. I told Stewart to let out a yell when he blocked. He knew the Basque shepherd cry, a weird mountain ululation, and he started it when Herman or Marlon came toward him. It added a bizarre note.

Room boys and maids had gathered along the perimeter, uncertain what they were watching, this slaughter should have a police permit. We didn't stop to explain, life's purpose had come down to winning this game.

The air was extremely hot and humid, after forty minutes our faces were fuchsia colored. Stewart and I had possession,

he snapped the ball to me, I dropped back, and he moved to
his right to take on the onrushing Herman, he drove his bald
head into Herman's stomach. "Arrghh," from Herman and
his eyeballs disconnected. I howled, I could see his corneas
searching for focus.

Stewart slid off his block and went sprinting—well, a
writer's version—downfield. Marlon had lain back to see the
play develop, now he came up swiftly to get me. I feathered a
spiral toward Stewart. He strode under it, varicosed legs
bending dangerously inward. The ball dropped into his arms,
he tucked it in and stepped over the goal line.

Highly amped, the four of us walked off the lawn. Marlon
and I exchanged hand slaps.

"Good game," he said.

"Yeah, what we needed." We were still in the battle, we
had not been movie star and aspiring producer out on that
quadrangle, we'd been Celt and Gael stepping on our own
entrails on the blood-soaked plain. Why? Why would a
touch-football game turn into a primordial battle? Something
between Marlon and me. There has been care and tenderness
between us, but competition is one of the deepest connections. Marlon had a bad knee and there was a real danger of
it coming apart. He was aware of it at first, but then it didn't
matter. The competition, all-out, unrestrained, mattered.

Thailand was to be next on the itinerary but we were coun-
seled more than once that if you're in Southeast Asia, you have
to stop in Hong Kong. Hong Kong was an open port then, a
place of Cold War intrigue. That didn't have specifically to do
with our film, but it excited our appetites. We went.

It was ritual for visiting celebrities to be entertained at the
home of Run Run Shaw and his wife, who were Hong Kong's

business royalty, she the social doyenne of the Crown Colony. Stewart wanted to organize his notes and Herman wanted to rest, so Marlon and I accepted the invitation to dinner. We felt like characters in a Graham Greene novel this sultry night. We were wearing white sharkskin suits we'd had made in a day and sitting on a deck looking out over the South China Sea.

Madame Shaw had invited two Chinese actresses, Li Li Wah and Sylvia Wu, as our dinner mates. They were revelations. Li Li Wah, with alluring eyes surrounded by a light delicate complexion, was my companion. A lithe beauty flowed through her spectacular figure, she managed to seem plump and lean at the same time. Peeking through her faultless British manners and fluid table talk was a subtle sensuality.

Marlon was finding appealing company in Sylvia Wu. The riveting thing about both of the ladies was the cheongsam they wore, a tight-fitting silk dress with a high mandarin collar. The collar gives a conservative appearance, but the bottom half of the dress is almost frankly sexual—slits on either side go to the upper thigh, leaving the legs exposed. These exposed legs were magnetic, Marlon and I widened our eyes at each other.

The evening began with gin, tonic, and shrimp flakes, lighter-than-air tempters that evaporated on our tongues. The dinner was an immersion in the mores and manners of Hong Kong. Madame Shaw was an empress, everything about the meal was patrician and precise—the serving of soups, refilling teacups, presentation of the next course, delivery of utensils. This was a way of doing things thousands of years old and it would not be changed during the reign of Madame Shaw.

When the meal was over Marlon and I invited our ladies for a drink at the Peninsula Hotel on the Kowloon side where we were staying. Rather formally they accepted. Their enthusiasm level was hard to read, but at least they were going with us. It's usual in Hong Kong to drink Scotch rather than wine through the meal. That's what Marlon and I had done and we were bombed.

When the Star Ferry docked on the Kowloon side, there were rickshaws lined up. We hired two of them to take us up the road to the hotel, we put our ladies in back and started in behind them.

"Wait," Marlon said. "I've got an idea."

He and I backed out of the vehicles then Marlon waved to the rickshaw boys to come out from between the pulling poles. He indicated they should get up into the seats beside the ladies. Toothy grins from the drivers, what was going on? Our dates looked chaste and uncomfortable as the dark-skinned and unkempt rickshaw boys sat beside them.

"Let's have a race, you and I pull the rickshaws," Marlon said.

Up came that competitive fire again, two guys looking for a new way to decide who's best.

"Great," I responded.

"Three blocks?"

"Fuck three blocks, to Chairman Mao's house. Okay, three blocks."

Marlon rehearsed Li Li and Sylvia in how to boom their commands for the start of the race. Then he and I got between the six-foot-long poles of the rickshaws. We'd seen hundreds of rickshaws being pulled through the Hong Kong streets, so we figured we knew how to do it, just run with a sort of gliding motion. It wasn't quite that simple. The key to pulling a rickshaw is balance, as we would soon find out.

Awkwardly I sidestepped in a circle to get next to Marlon for the start. When we were lined up he waved to the girls and they, in their tinkling Oriental sopranos, bellowed: "Ready! (Leady!) Set! Go!!"

We leaped forward. I immediately shot to the right, stopped to correct, then blasted too far to the left, I was heading right for the wharf we'd just left. Marlon was in a similar tangle. We both got straightened out and were parallel again and began legging it for real down Nathan Road. We were breathing like horses, slit-eyed, sweating through our dress shirts, and swiftly picking up momentum. The rickshaws banged and bounced behind us. Sylvia and Li Li, totally into it, shouted exhortations. The rickshaw boys got the spirit, too, and in Cantonese hollered, "Run, you pale-skinned assholes." Clacking down the street like ostriches, Marlon and I were each determined to win.

Rickshaws are cranky to slow down from a walk, but if you, inexperienced, try to halt one at a full gallop, you're likely to snap a leg off at the ankle. When the light suddenly turned red on the avenue ahead, dense with crossing traffic, the encouraging yells from our dates died in their throats. Marlon and I had the same reaction, we dug in our feet and leaned back. Feet don't get traction at that velocity and with that much mass behind them. The attempt not only brought no slowing, it ripped our feet off the road and sent us yawing into the air. We cantered zigzag toward the intersection like figures in an undercranked film. Everything on the sides streamed into a blur: awed onlookers with their mouths open, neon signs in Chinese, children pointing, screams of alarm. The boulevard we were approaching at missile speed was thick with buses, diesel-powered lorries, taxis, motorcycles, bicycles.

The girls' screams were a wail of death. The rickshaw boys vaulted out—getting hit by an eight-ton truck was a better deal than what we were headed for. Marlon and I came flying into the intersection, into a maelstrom of horns, yells, locked-up brakes, skidding tires. I swerved left to try to miss the Range Rover coming on my right and in one second I was on my back.

Hong Kong police at that time had to be six feet or taller. A Chinese cop, seeming unreal at at six-four, grabbed Marlon's rickshaw and ran it alongside a bus till friction brought it to a halt. Two other giants helped us out from under the poles. They assisted the ladies to their feet. Li Li and Sylvia had been badly bounced around but miraculously were unhurt. Courteously but sternly the police told us how close we'd come to dying. We nodded, two schoolboys. Bruised and ashen, we shook hands with the rickshaw boys and gave them some money. That gave us big face with the onlookers, cheers went up.

A string ensemble was playing in the Peninsula Hotel's palm court, our dates were calm and gorgeous once more, and no one amid that British orderliness could have guessed from what dramatic circumstances we had just returned. That shared event brought the four of us together in a way no evening of elegant dancing could have. We laughed and were amazed as we reviewed what we'd done. A lovely intimacy was produced.

In the lounge at Kai Tak Airport the next morning Marlon and I looked back on the trip thus far. Here we were in the Orient, the dawn coming up like thunder from China across the bay—we were in the middle of what we'd read about as boys. What lay ahead?

For one thing, Marlon didn't make the tour with us. After

Hong Kong he went to Bali then back to California. It seemed sad to Stewart and me, almost like desertion; we were supposed to have this experience together then come home and put it into a film. Marlon seemed to be taking a step away from the project, from responsibility for it. I would see this pattern repeated more than once in the future.

However, in fairness it can be said that there was no specific need for Marlon to go through every one of those countries. He wasn't going to write the script, he wasn't going to direct the picture, keeping an objective view was arguably more valuable than being along for every mile of the research.

Also, I felt that while we should have fun wherever we could, our work came first. I saw myself as responsible for our mission's success. Stewart and I shared that code, but that aspect of me could have been irritating to Marlon.

Whenever, in the long history of our relationship, I became the authority figure—producer or director or head of the company—things could get slippery. It might be Marlon's reflexive reaction to authority, it might stem from our different experiences in military school. Though Marlon and I were both rebellious, I was successful in the military structure, I became the ranking officer in the battalion. At Shattuck, Marlon's conflict with the administration got him expelled. That increased his dislike of authority and intensified his feeling that he was an outsider.

Stewart worked hard on his story when we returned from Asia. He called it *Tiger on a Kite* and finished it in ten weeks.

Perhaps Marlon didn't picture as vividly as Stewart and I the sequences Stewart had written, but he didn't like the treatment. He wasn't concerned with the locale or the accuracy with which the UN was portrayed, he was concerned with the story and his role.

Stewart had done hard work, good work, but his story was a first assault, it would have to grow through future stages. Now was the time for Marlon to lend his talent to the project, help to shape it.

It was a complex situation. Stewart felt Marlon's negative reaction came not from a thoughtful evaluation of the work but from guilt that he had not participated in the research. We were abroad eight weeks, Stewart noted, and of that time Marlon spent two and a half hours in actual field research— at the barrio of Santo Tomas outside Manila.

Marlon didn't only reject Stewart's story, he concocted a new one. Stewart's indignation was deep. Marlon hadn't read Stewart's comprehensive research notes. If he had, Stewart said, he could suggest alternatives that came from the true picture of what happened, that was the right way to do it, that would fulfill the reason for making the trip. Stewart opposed Marlon inventing a story basically unconnected to the research. In a memo to me Stewart wrote:

Knowing that we might find a treasure trove of material in Indonesia, Marlon skirted his responsibility and indulged himself by going to Bali. I think he was following an old neurotic pattern, to test the patience of others to its limit with the hope of being called to task and punished. His denunciation of his country at all press conferences was further testing of our patience.

The long memo ended:

> Maybe Marlon's role should be delimited for him, he is first,
> foremost and ONLY an actor—albeit the best alive today. He
> must examine his mistrust of all directors, all writers, in the
> light of his mistrust of himself. It is mistrust, not trust, which
> makes him feel uniquely qualified to write for himself and to
> direct himself. He will be ruined if he continues under this
> unreasonable illusion.

Intelligent words. But there was substance on Marlon's
side, too. He had sharp perceptions about his character and a
couple of strong story ideas. Marlon showed something
else—generosity. When he and Stewart could find no way forward, Marlon offered to pay Stewart to write his story then
help him get it made with another actor.

Marlon made another important point—fidelity to research
doesn't create compelling movies, drama does. In this case,
with our responsibility to the UN to be accurate, Stewart and
I may have been too concerned with fact and not enough, at
least at the beginning, with the necessary conflicts. Still, you
don't produce the whole screenplay the first time you write
the treatment.

Our difficulties were not only with *Tiger on a Kite*. Marlon's dissatisfaction with the writing was understandable but
his solutions were worrisome. Rather than give his thoughts
to the writers and work with them, he wanted to take over
the writing himself. Marlon is quick, with a keen sense of
drama, but there's a question as to whether he has the discipline to get all the way through a screenplay and the subse-
quent drafts.

Marlon left for Japan to film *Sayonara*. While there, he was going to write his version of our western. He wanted me to go and work with him on the script. I could see that this would be terrific fun, but it probably wouldn't move our business forward. I told him I felt I had to be in California to ensure Pennebaker's production schedule.

I hoped Marlon would be diligent, I hoped he'd write something good, but I wasn't optimistic. Getting a picture produced by Pennebaker wasn't a necessity for him. If his script worked, fine, if it didn't, also fine, there would be something else to do. Marlon wasn't interested in nor did he really grasp the financial reasons for having his own production company, so whether or not Pennebaker was successful was not a major issue to him. I was beginning to see that in reality we were competing like every other company for his services.

While Marlon was in Japan, Mr. Freeman called me in again. Were we for sure going to start production by the May 15 date we'd given him? I said we had every intention of making that date. That wasn't the answer he wanted.

"Englund, we're doing everything you boys want, we did that research trip, paid the writers, that's fine, that's why we're here. But, Englund, I've got to get a picture out of this. Now you tell me exactly to the day when we're going to get that picture. Is it May fifteenth?"

"Both Marlon and his father have agreed to the date," I said, "there's no question about that. And we've got the script of *Yellow Leg* ready to go. The real question is what we get from Marlon; as you know he's working on his own version of our western in Japan. For everybody's sake the first picture we make has to be the right picture for Marlon. He's too precious an asset to use badly."

"The best picture for Marlon is the one you all decide you're going to put your best into, that's what I think. You got three or four good ideas, I know them, they're good. You put on your war bonnet and decide to make one of them, that is the way to make the best picture for Marlon and for Paramount. And let me mention something they don't talk a lot about in this town, but where I come from it's important—integrity. I can tell you when we made this deal I looked it over very carefully and I knew it was going to cost some money, but I said we're going to do it and we're going to be honorable partners. Anytime you think we're not or I'm not, you come in here and tell me. I want you and Marlon to have all the success in the world, Englund, I want to help you have it. Along with it, if you don't mind considering an old Southern way of thinking, I want you all to be honorable partners, too."

I agreed with Mr. Freeman. He had been an honorable partner. We should be honorable partners, too.

In Japan, Marlon was fighting his interior devils. In a long letter he told me he was trying to erase his suspicions about women, his defenses against loving and being loved. In part the letter reads:

> *I have moved into a Japanese room in the hotel and the exquisite simplicity of it lends itself perfectly to my urge to contemplate . . . I'm experiencing loneliness, distrust, whistling hate, love impulses, soaring esteem for courage, the need for simplicity. I've finished reading Eric Fromm's* The Art of Loving *and found my own shocking image on every other page. I'm currently reading* The Outsider *and again finding myself mirrored. I am not a believer, and a life without faith obliges*

me to live on the land, hiding by day and running by night. I
realize more and more that to try to establish my identity
through externals, i.e. sex, position, people, career is danger-
ous and hopeless.

Later he says:

I met Truman Capote the other day, he has become a Zen
Buddhist and is now studying to take orders. Truman said he
would like me to meet him and have a talk about his experi-
ences which I'm burning to do.

The last is ironic. Shortly after writing this letter, Marlon
met again with Capote. They did have a long and personal
talk, which Marlon understood to be private. But Capote
published almost the whole conversation in *The New Yorker*.
Marlon felt betrayed.

At the end of the letter Marlon is tired and says:

I'll write you another letter that concerns itself with the
mundane and earthbound details of who is Buster Crabbe's
agent and who was the best chiropodist in 1860.

Love to you, Mar.

P.S. Sayonara: a darkling plain where ignorant armies clash
by night.

Just before Marlon went to Japan, I had been asked by Jean
Dalrymple, head of the City Center in New York, to direct
the revival there of *Brigadoon*, by Alan Lerner and Fritz
Loewe. Both Marlons said that since we'd be in a slack

period while *Sayonara* was being filmed, it would be a good idea to do it. Lerner and Loewe's *My Fair Lady* was a behemoth hit and this revival would be the first production of one of their shows since *My Fair Lady* had opened.

A couple of days before I was to leave for New York, Marlon returned from Japan with his treatment. He called it *A Burst of Vermillion*. It was 312 pages long.

Senior, Jay Kanter (Marlon's agent), and I read it, as did others at the agency. All opinions were the same. Though there were interesting elements in it, the writing was undisciplined, the story incoherent and rambling. It could certainly not be turned into a screenplay for shooting in the middle of May.

In my memo to Marlon about *A Burst of Vermillion*, I cheered his staying with the work and writing at such length. But the large number of pages, I said, did not mean the treatment was overwritten; I believed it to be underwritten in terms of character and story structure. I said that what he wrote for himself should be given the same scrutiny as what was written for him by anybody else. We should not use a different standard because he was the author.

The morning of the day I was going to New York, Senior called: Marlon wanted to have a meeting after work about his treatment. I said okay but I had to be on the plane to New York at ten forty-five. I wanted to make sure that Senior, Jay, and I were in agreement about what we were going to say to Marlon about his treatment. I suggested the three of us meet for lunch.

At lunch we reviewed Marlon's treatment and again were unanimous in our opinions. It would be wasteful and profitless to do any more work on it. Marlon was likely to try postponing the production date again, we could all see that, and all agreed it would be wrong for every reason to let it happen. Pennebaker should make good on its commitment to Frank Freeman and Paramount. *Yellow Leg* could turn into a great first picture.

That night, upstairs in Marlon's bedroom in the house on Laurel View Drive, we met. Marlon had come from the studio, where he was filming interiors for *Sayonara*. He was in makeup and the uniform of an army lieutenant, though he'd taken off his jacket and tie. He sat on his bed, against the headboard, we in chairs facing him.

He began with a long statement—he didn't believe in *Yellow Leg*, he did believe in *A Burst of Vermillion*. He'd read it again and he liked it.

"It's not perfect, it's not finished, but it's good. I think it's better than maybe the three of you think it is, it has a character I want to play, it says something I want to say. I don't think I should do a script I don't believe in, my first commitment has to be to myself. I'm not going to do *Yellow Leg* because it's ordinary and there's no reason to do it except that we've got a production date. We should get behind *A Burst of Vermillion* and make that when it's ready. George, you can help me write it, we can make it a good script."

He stopped and looked at me. "What do you think?"

"I'd rather hear your father first," I said.

Senior lifted his eyebrows. "Well . . . I think, I think Bud's saying something that's—he's got a point. He believes in his script maybe there's awm more to it than awm we . . . we thought, I think we should take another look, consider what Bud's said . . ."

Marlon was impatient, he wasn't greatly interested in his father's opinion. He turned back to me.

"George?"

"I'd like to hear what Jay has to say."

Marlon looked to Jay. "Jay, what do you think?"

Jay moved in his chair. "Well, we've got to think about what we're dealing with, we're dealing with Marlon's company, he's the head of it. Our opinions may be different than his, but Senior is right, I think we've got to reevaluate our plans. Marlon knows what character he wants to play, I think we have to go along with that. We'll just tell Paramount we're not going to do *Yellow Leg,* we have to postpone. They'll survive."

For me, their two statements were a death knell. Night had fallen on my hopes for our company. Marlon looked to me again.

"Okay, having heard your father and Jay, I can be brief, Mar. First, I'm the only one in this room who's telling you the truth. It's possible that someday your treatment could become a good screenplay, but that would take months, if it ever got done at all. Jay knows it, your father knows it, we've discussed it thoroughly. Second, we've made a commitment to Paramount to start production on May fifteenth. We can do that, we're ready to make a good film, maybe something a lot better than that. We looked at all our options before we made the commitment. I believe we should have kept our word. We seem to be in the business of *not* making motion pictures. I don't want to do that, so that's all for me."

"What does that mean?" Marlon said.

"I'm leaving the company."

Senior and Jay sat up and said I shouldn't quit, that would

be crazy. Senior said go to New York, direct the show, don't decide something in anger. I wasn't angry, I said, I was calm.

I hadn't expected Senior and Jay to change so completely, but when they did, I knew it was over.

Marlon didn't say much at first. He listened to the discussion among us. Then he, too, said I shouldn't quit.

I had about six thousand dollars in the bank, no job now, was being paid scale for directing *Brigadoon*. I had two kids and George Jr. would be born in three months. But there was no question in my mind that leaving Pennebaker was the right thing to do.

I don't know how well Marlon remembers that meeting, I don't know whether he thinks I was right or wrong, but I believe that my decision that night did more to anchor his trust in me than anything else ever has.

5

—

In the bedroom in Marlon's guesthouse, five brief months before his death, my thoughts drift back to Anna, then to other women in Marlon's life. He was magnetic even when he was poor and studying at the New School in New York, but add the corona of stardom to him and you have an irresistible force. In his golden days Marlon was simply, overwhelmingly attractive.

You're a woman, you've just met Marlon. He's not what you expected, he's interesting and interested in you. He asks about the details of your life, where you grew up, if your parents are still married, how many brothers and sister you have. He's disarmingly frank. "When did you last sleep with someone?" he asks. He is fascinating in a way no one else

has ever been. When he takes your hand it is sensual, you are bewitched by the way he explores it. His aura suggests an erotica of different aromas, different vulgarities, different safaris, you will go with him somewhere you have not been before. He has not yet fondled your body, he is fondling your mind.

You are cheerful that when your secret self was asked to be revealed, you could yield it to him so promptly. He has awakened you to possibilities inside you that lay unaroused before his touch. To be in the care of such a one, that he should know you in so complete a way, notice even the tiniest hair the sun catches on your neck, oh, divine life. You would die for it.

So, when he has vanished, life has a bleakness unmatched. He could not *not* have cared, he took so much time with you, he took your most secret parts in his hands, loved you . . . it's not possible he doesn't telephone, too ghastly that he doesn't answer your calls. He gave you the private number, you shared his bedroom, you were part of his inner temple. You live in despair now, so awakened yesterday, so helpless a Galatea today.

To find a way back into his world you accept humiliation, you become one of several. You have no fixed place, you are nervously on the cusp, where you may be nudged off because of an infraction you didn't know you were committing. Your breath is bad, your humor is weak, your vaginal cleansing is ineffective, the backseat of your car looks like a garbage bin, in some way you either are or are about to be hateful. But you stay, craving the soothing, the stroking of your mind, the exploring of your body. You stay and the memory that your life once had another purpose—to be a dancer or a writer— recedes and blurs.

Marlon is good in the short term, all his charm and humor are in play. In the long pull they're replaced by suspicion and the certainty he will be betrayed. However alluring a woman may seem, Marlon knows he's looking at someone whose frailty, like that of his mother, will inevitably surface. Better not to wait, manipulate it into view now.

He and I used to be similar in that way and we learned from each other, watched each other, tried the other's techniques. A description of what one of us might have done serves for the other as well.

The woman is thirty-two, very attractive, very adroit socially. She has a charming laugh that shows her teeth well, she uses it often. Marlon has noticed, it's the kind of social passport he fastens on, he sees the vulnerability behind it.

"Why did you laugh just then?" he says.

It's said nicely; still, the question is blunt. The woman covers with what always works so well for her; she laughs, splendidly.

"I don't know, maybe because you're funny," she says.

"I'm funny?"

"Mmm-hmm, you make me laugh." The laugh comes again, lovely, musical.

"What about me makes you laugh? Is my hair on fire?"

She laughs. "No, of course not."

"Saliva running down my chin?"

She laughs again, but less. "No."

"Then what's making you laugh?"

"Isn't it all right to laugh?"

"Of course. But generally there's a cause. You said I was funny, but I don't remember being funny. Tell me what was funny."

"Nothing, I guess."

"Nothing. Well, that makes you a happy person, you can laugh when nothing funny's happened . . . could you laugh right now?"

She feels the hostility, it shows in him now. The panicked voice inside her says, "For God's sake, don't laugh, it will be total humiliation, confirmation of your emptiness." But in times of uncertainty that lilting, appealing laugh is her go-to strength. Helplessly she parts her lips and into Marlon's cold countenance she laughs; the attractive laugh that shows her teeth well.

He watches, his dark eyes laying her to waste.

"You changed color when you laughed then."

She's in flight, her composure is gone, her face is distraught. How did she lose the things that are engaging about her, where has fled her self-confidence, why is she about to cry?

Why is she about to cry? Because she has slipped into the embrace of America's greatest pound-for-pound woman punisher.

Perhaps there is a new woman in whom Marlon is interested. Once the affair starts, it won't be long before his mistrust shoulders in. In a conversation about her past affairs, he might center on a brief one she's mentioned.

"Marlon," she'll say laughing. "It was one night way back when, you and I didn't even know each other."

"No, of course we didn't. But when you think about it, everything we do means something. That one-nighter has some meaning even today."

"Don't be silly; it was two years ago and it didn't mean anything then."

"It was your friend's husband."

"They'd gotten a divorce. He was broken up by it and seemed terribly sad and . . ."

"And what?" He waits. "You had to rescue him by fucking him?"

"Don't say it that way. God." She's distraught. "He was a friend, I suppose it was part pity, part—I don't know what."

"It was part sex, wasn't it?"

"Yes. But I don't see why we need to talk about it."

"Did you come?"

"God, what is this about?"

"If we're talking about it, let's be sure we get the details right. Did you?"

"I don't know. Yes, I'm sure I did."

"Okay, so you invested, you gave yourself."

She feels raped, violated. "I fucked him, Marlon, I did what you do when you fuck somebody, all of what you do, everything you do." It comes out in a torrent of anger and humiliation and protest.

"Okay. All I'm saying is it wasn't nothing."

"That's not all you're saying, you're saying it was dirty."

"Was it?"

"Of course not. What is going on? Why are you doing this?"

Marlon shines compassion and condemnation on her. "Because the best way to know about the future is to know the past."

She feels a darkening and she's right. He moves to the possibility she'll have an affair in the future. He develops the idea, imagines how it might happen, even seems to suggest it, even to consider its benefits . . . until finally it does happen.

Then, like a physician who's stood a long bedside vigil, he'll close his valise and walk out into the gray morning, purified in the knowledge that she went out and fucked someone else.

Now that she's fallen, he doesn't need to be vengeful, he can even be understanding. He knows human peccadilloes. Later he might even fuck her again, why not, it's a body with familiar curves and temperature and now she's been defanged.

Among women, Marlon does not suspend use of his arsenal of social shocks, one of them being an ability to fart at will. In a meeting, in mixed company, anywhere, with utter disregard for social norms, he will launch one. He's aware of the horror others feel about farting in public, it's their consternation after he farts that interests him.

There is a Japanese woman in Marlon's life, she is beautiful with a fine sense of chic. But along with her sophistication she is extremely shy, she colors when attention is called to her, she covers her face when she laughs. Marlon is charmed by her embarrassments.

He and she, call her Sono, were in an elevator in Century City. Not long into the ascent, amid the subdued elevator conversation, Marlon farted audibly. He acted startled and leaped sideways—where did that come from? Then he fixed on her a look of disbelief; she, his beautiful flower from Japan, had done it. He bent to her and in a stage whisper said, "Not in the elevator, darling, not in the United States." Crimson, mortified, her hand covering her mouth, she stared at the floor.

He put his arm around her and gave her an understanding squeeze—we'll just put it behind us. While the passengers waited in dread for the odor of the fart to measure up to its audio quality, Marlon rapped out a second one, brutal, something out of a stall in a a truck stop in Enid, Oklahoma. He whirled to her, trying to make a loving smile, but unable to hide his dismay—darling, you really must stop.

This was not just humiliation for the poor young lady, it was catastrophic beyond belief, the worst possible thing, loss of face.

Marlon told me about the incident while Sono was there. She was embarrassed to hear it retold but laughed as I laughed. I think she understands it to be Marlon's version of loving fun.

One night some weeks after that event he and Sono and I were sitting before the fire in his bedroom. He started rubbing his middle finger as if it were sore. He offered it to Sono, saying he'd stubbed it and it needed to be pulled out.

"What?"

"This knuckle is jammed from where I hit it on the stove and it needs to be pulled out. Could you do it?"

Uncertainly, Sono took his finger, studied it, then pulled.

"That's not quite it, you have to get it to snap," Marlon said. "Here, let me show you." He took her middle finger in his hand. "Take hold of it like this and yank it hard."

Sono was reluctant to be so energetic with a bruised finger. She took it again and pulled harder. Nope, his face said, still not enough.

"Here, this'll help," he said. He rose and pulled her up beside him. "Raise it over your head then pull it down with all your might, get your whole body into it."

She took his finger again.

"Give it everything you've got."

Committed now, she raised Marlon's finger to head height and whipped it down with all her might.

Out of a kelp bed came Marlon's fart.

"Whoa, God, thanks." He smiled to her. "I feel a whole lot better."

Sono's large dark eyes stared. "How could you do something so unspeakable?" they asked.

She was so hurt Marlon didn't dare laugh, even though her reaction made it funnier.

"Sorry, Sono. I think I was a little pent up from worrying about my finger. It did really hurt and that pull helped a ton."

She was disgusted with what he had done. We watched TV awhile, then Marlon shook the fingers on his hand to indicate pain. Sono looked over. Marlon bit his lip to indicate the pain in his finger was bad. He held the finger up.

"Don't be rude, Marlon."

"Rude? I'm not being rude, this is killing me." He held the finger out.

"No, I don't help again."

"Why?"

"Don't make stupid."

"Because I made a joke when you pulled my finger?"

"Not joke, you make horrible . . ." She gestured to the air.

"I wouldn't do that again," Marlon protested with Frank Morgan indignation. "My finger hurts too bad."

She looked unmovable. On the other hand she wanted to believe. "Marlon, you so naughty, how somebody trust?"

He spoke quietly, there was hurt in his voice. "What are you saying, Sono?"

"I don't believe."

"Hearing you say that is worse than the pain in my finger. Worse than any pain I'll ever have."

Sono couldn't bear that kind of talk. She got up. "Give me finger."

He rose and held it out so she could get a grip.

"Finger really hurt, Marlon?"

"Really hurts bad."

"Same way? Quick?"

"Same way, just snap the hell out of it."

She raised his finger over her head and this time pulled out all the stops; she hurled herself into a mighty downstroke. The fart of the ages brayed through the room.

Her violated eyes couldn't believe that he had done it again and *she* had done it again.

She wheeled toward the kitchen, hiccuping with emotion.

It was one of those instances where in spite of what your brain says, you go along with Marlon's insane premise. He couldn't possibly be going through all this, you reason, just for a practical joke, no adult would do that. So you act as if his finger really is out of joint. And again you make the mistake you're not entitled to make—you know better, you know Marlon will go to absolutely any length to get you to go along.

Why Sono would ever speak to him again was the question. I think she decided to take on this role of the embarrassed Oriental because Marlon liked it. She became, in a way, his straight man. I think Sono understood more than she let Marlon know. I believe she loves Marlon to this minute.

There was another woman in Marlon's life at the time, a movie star. A lot of his complexities came into play with her. Their relationship was emotional, worrisome, and often painful.

I picked her up at the doctor's office one afternoon in Beverly Hills. She had had an abortion. Abortions were illegal then and Marlon and she had asked if I would go to the office after the surgery and take her home. I said of course. I had never realized the trauma that goes with abortion before that day.

She was drawn and shaken and perhaps in shock when she came out of the doctor's office. I remember most the tears and look of almost unbearable sadness. I hadn't thought, and maybe Marlon hadn't, how much she wanted that baby, how agonizing it was to have yielded it up.

I assisted her into the car, chatting quietly and hoping I was helpful on the ride to her house, I walked her to her front door. Just after we'd said good-bye and she'd closed the door, she opened it again, she'd forgotten to give me something. I went back. A gift for bringing her home, a pad of "Ex Libris" stickers with my name printed on them to put in my books. As she had planned for the pain and woe of that day, she included a remembrance for me. I've thought that she wanted everything associated with that day to be proper so that when she looked back on it she would be able to find some order and sense in it. I still have the "Ex Libris" stickers. I come across them every so often and every time I do I'm stilled by the sadness I remember on her face.

In 1958, *The Ugly American* was published. It was written by a retired navy captain, William Lederer, and a professor of political theory at the University of California and former Rhodes scholar, Eugene Burdick. Part fiction, part nonfiction, the book contained both essays and short stories about U.S. Foreign Service personnel in Asia.

It told that they lived in their own communes, known derisively among their hosts as golden ghettos, in the capital cities. Too many Americans exploited their PX privileges, almost none learned the language of the country, few ventured to the hinterlands. American officials in these Oriental countries were, for the most part, ignorant of the aspirations of the people, their feelings and their needs. Ignorant, too, of the pressure being put on them by the Soviet Union to join the Communist bloc. *Ignorance* was the word; hundreds of millions of U.S. dollars were lost in futile aid projects in Asia.

It was the right document appearing at the right time; America devoured *The Ugly American* and made it number one on the *New York Times* bestseller list for twenty-six weeks. An aspiring presidential candidate thought the book so vivid, so vital to the national interest, that he sent a copy to every member of Congress, saying it was must reading. It was the sort of bumptious thing Jack Kennedy was doing a lot of in the run-up to the 1960 Democratic Convention; he wanted to be the candidate.

Because of our research trip through Southeast Asia, I was familiar with much that was in the book. The incidents cited were often the kind of experiences we had found.

I could see that in *The Ugly American* was the stuff of a good picture for Marlon, it could be the finale we didn't get to at Pennebaker.

A high price was being asked for the film rights, but so far no studio had acquired them. It would not be an easy screenplay to write, as nobody in Hollywood had much knowledge of the subject.

Burdick and Lederer were in town and I arranged to meet them for breakfast. I wanted to persuade them I was the man to produce the movie of their book, that my experiences in Southeast Asia were congruent with what they had written. They said that just before they'd come to breakfast, their agent had called to say Universal had decided to buy the film rights. They said we don't know the movie business, George, but to us you seem like a good candidate, so we'll recommend you to Ed Muhl and Mel Tucker, the studio heads.

The recommendation helped; Muhl and Tucker asked to meet with me. They were surprised that anyone from the industry had had such extensive experience in that part of the world. They asked if Marlon was interested. I said maybe— he'd wanted to do the UN project and there were a lot of similarities. I said I would try to bring him in, but I couldn't guarantee anything.

Stewart Stern was engaged to write and I to produce *The Ugly American*.

In early 1960, in the Senate Office Building, I met with Senator John Kennedy, who was such a strong advocate of the book. His energy was immediately impressive. His Down East accent hit you right away. His interest in the book and his knowledge of the subject were real. The problems with the Foreign Service had to be corrected, he said. American diplomats needed aggressive schooling. He felt the movie could help bring the matter home to the American people. I outlined what we planned to do with the story, the theme of the picture; he said it sounded excellent.

He said he'd watch our progress, and if I needed any help along the way to call him, he wanted to see *The Ugly American* made. I thanked him and we ended the meeting.

One last thing impressed me about Senator Kennedy—the distinguished cut of his suit. When we did the film, I had

Marlon's suits made by Jack Kennedy's tailor, Sam Harris, in New York.

In February of 1961, we hit a devastating problem in the script: one of the key elements in the book, and the keel of our screenplay, was erroneous. In the book, Homer Atkins, an American engineer, notices two things in the Southeast Asian country he's helping. One, there isn't enough rice; two, there are a lot of bicycles. He invents a simple way for the bicycles to be converted into water pumps. The rider, remaining stationary, uses leg power to bring water from the stream into the rice field. Yankee ingenuity, not a lot of heedless spending, one of the most captivating illustrations in the book. It was horse puckey.

The temperature was ninety-seven degrees and the humidity the same when a toothless headman in an up-country village in Thailand said to me that if all the men in his village lined up and pissed into their rice fields at the same time, it wouldn't dent the irrigation problem, but it would do more than the bicycle pump we'd described to him. He pointed up the hill and our guide translated: You see up there where the rice planting begins . . . well, we need more rice in this village, we would plant higher . . . the reason the planting starts there is because that's where the water comes out. Rice has to be grown underwater—*and* the water has to be moving. He laughed again at the idea of the bicycle pumps. The script was wreckage.

Burdick and Lederer had leaped into prominence as experts on Southeast Asia because they'd gone into the boonies, talked to the peasants, the farmers with real thoroughness. The bicycle pump may have been the one thing they hadn't checked out. They wrote well and their thesis was correct, but this central episode was not. Burdick told me later he thought Stewart and I had probably gone farther, stayed longer, and learned more about Southeast Asia than he and Lederer had.

Activity on the film stopped while the studio decided whether to continue or abandon the project. A year and a half of my life was invested in *The Ugly American*. I tried to persuade Muhl and Tucker that there was a good solution to the problem, I'd thought it out. They listened, but it was a risky picture to begin with and they had to think carefully about it.

I sat alone at home that night and in the Gorky-like melancholy my mind went back to the beginning of Jack Kennedy's campaign for the presidency. His first day of campaigning began in a town in northern Wisconsin. It was cold, there weren't many people on the street, and of those that were, many were indifferent to the young candidate.

"Hello, I'm John Kennedy, I want to be president of the United States, I'd like your vote." He'd walk up, hand extended. You didn't feel a prairie fire starting. But from that unmemorable beginning he'd gone all the way to the White House.

The fact that Kennedy was Catholic was one of his big problems; there had never been a Catholic president. He was quizzed by a panel of television journalists—how could he reconcile his Catholic beliefs with the separation of church and state demanded by the Constitution. Kennedy was good, he quoted the Constitution verbatim. He said his religion was private and it would in no way influence his performance in office. Both personally and as president, he would be vigilant in defense of this most defining aspect of American government, the separation of church and state. It was inspiring; that's what you do, approach your problems as if they're opportunities. I was inspired by him that night. I made a new charge at the studio heads and shortly after they gave us a go-ahead on the rewrite. Stewart finished it in twelve weeks.

The role of Ambassador MacWhite had been written with Marlon in mind; now it was time to see if he would do it. He was in New York. I called him.

"Stew's finished the script, Mar, I'd like you to read it."

"Good. Send it, I'll call you right away."

We spoke during the next ten days, but he didn't read the script. Maddening time for a producer—if the star says no, you take the bruise and go on, but if the star says yes, the world is turned around. You've got a living project, you're going to make a movie, what you joined up for.

Muhl and Tucker decided I'd better go to New York and get a yes or no. Marlon said it was great I was coming. It was. We were out every night, sometimes just him and me, sometimes with others, always fun, always fascinating. And no discussion about the script. We'd start to talk about it, then he'd say how anxious he was to read it, then the phone would ring or the girls would arrive and I'd close up my sample case. I'd been there five days.

"Mar, you've got to read the script. The studio is not going to finance me here through Lent."

"I'll read it tonight."

"Okay, for sure."

"We'll have dinner, then I'll go back and read it."

We went to dinner. With France Nuyen. At a Chinese restaurant. We had a great time double-talking poor France, whose English was limited. Probably because she didn't understand, she thought it was as funny as we did. It was after midnight when Marlon and I walked up to his building.

"How could it have gotten this late, how could I have assisted in you not reading the script again?" I said.

"We had a good dinner, I'll read it. Come on in."

"No, Mar, I want you to read the script."

"I will, come in for a while."

"If I come in we'll talk. I'm going to the hotel and sit by the phone."

"Just come in, I want to talk about the script a little."

"Five minutes."

He'd rented a garden apartment on East Fifty-third Street for the several months he'd be in New York. The living room opened in the back on a beautiful garden with a scattering of trees. It was a warm night and Marlon opened the garden doors.

"Hang on a sec, be right out," he said.

He came out in a Japanese kimono and was tying his obi. I was in an armchair, he came over to me, put the script in my lap, sat on the sofa opposite, and pushed back into a comfortable position.

"All right, read it to me," he said.

"Read it?"

Marlon was my friend, he was also America's greatest living actor—how would you read a script to him? Do the female parts in a soprano, do the Oriental roles like Charlie Chan?

"That's the best way, I'll get more out of it, Georgie."

My mother once told me an old show-business saying: "Make a good bluff, then make the bluff good." I thought about it then opened the script. It was ten after two when I started.

" 'Fade-in. Jungle Country—Day. A jeep is moving along the black-top coils of Freedom Road, journeying higher through the Asian rain forest. At the wheel is Homer Atkins, a leathery engineer dressed in suntans and an old safari hat. He has a craggy, lined face. Because of this face the Asian people he works with refer to him affectionately as the ugly American.' "

Two men facing each other through the early-morning hours, one reading and gesturing, the other still and listening. And listen Marlon did, to every word. I was doing my best to bring out the drama in the script and I soon forgot the acting supremacy of my audience. Both of us became absorbed, both unaware of how little or how much time went by.

When I came to the word *fade-out,* dawn had arrived, birds were making their first noises in the garden, my voice was hoarse and at whisper level. Marlon's eyes peered at me as they had through the whole reading. He was wide-awake.

"Good, Georgie. Some things I want to talk about in the script, but I'm going to do the picture. Get some sleep, we'll get at it again tomorrow."

6

When the Vatican cardinals have elected a new pope, the white smoke from the burning ballots rises from the chimney in the Sistine Chapel and the Cardinal Camerlengo comes out onto the balcony overlooking St. Peter's Square. He proclaims to the gathered thousands, *"Gaudium magnum, habemus papam."* Glorious tidings, we have a pope.

I wanted a crier to do that at Universal. "Glorious tidings, we're making a movie."

Two months before we were to start shooting *The Ugly American,* there was worry about Marlon's weight. He was twenty or twenty-five pounds heavier than he should be, he didn't look like a movie star, the studio said. Marlon agreed to lose weight. But he showed no measurable change. The studio finally said if Marlon didn't lose at least fifteen pounds, they would not start the picture. Since I was not only

the producer but also Marlon's friend, I was to watch his eating and try to get him to reduce.

Arthur Loew, a prominent producer and one of our chums, gave frequent parties. Stewart would always be there, and Joan Collins, Paul Newman and Joanne Woodward, Marlon, a mixture of other stars, writers, directors.

Arthur lived in the Hollywood Hills and had a magnificent view of the city. At a party at his house one night, Marlon's gastronomical restraint deserved applause. He not only refused food but turned down a margarita because it had sugar in it. Sometime later in the evening, somebody, I forget who, told me I should look in the kitchen, something important was going on. I quickly scanned the room for Marlon; he wasn't there. He is a modern Scarlet Pimpernel, he can just melt out of a crowd.

I went to the kitchen door and eased it open. The lights were off, but Marlon was silhouetted against the window, bellied up to the sink. A whole pie was in one hand, a quart of milk in the other. His right cheek was bulging as he worked a mammoth slab of the dessert down.

"Caught," I said from the doorway.

"No, uh-uh, you don't get any points for that, I knew you'd get your tapir nose out and look for me." He didn't turn around, kept munching and looking out the window.

"You knew it and performed this shameful act anyway. You thought you'd get away with it."

"If I wanted to hide the pie and the milk, would I eat it in the kitchen?"

I walked up to him. "You are busted. You may make one phone call to your attorney before you are taken to Ed Muhl's office and weighed."

"Fuck 'em, you didn't see anything." He broke off a piece of the pie and handed me it to me.

I took it and chewed beside him. Hollywood was all lit up below us. In fact, Hollywood was all around, stars and executives in the other room, this was the movie business. There was that sense of expectation as you got closer to the shooting date. But the problem of Marlon's weight had to be attended to.

"Mar, put down the rest of the pie."

"Why?"

"*Why?*"

"Yeah."

"No good reason, just the nine thousand calories."

"What do you care, look how skinny you are."

"I'm not playing the role."

"What's that got to do with it?

He kept talking and stalling until he finished the pie. The last bite was in his mouth and he was flushing it down with the milk. He put the empty bottle down and belched. "Shall we join the ladies?" he said in a delicate Mayfair accent.

Marlon lost weight, not the fifteen pounds the studio had demanded but enough for a compromise.

When it came time to choose a director for the picture, Marlon said to me, "I think you ought to direct it. You do it." It was an enormous thing, a second opportunity provided by Marlon. Though I hadn't directed a film before, the studio accepted me as director.

We shot locations in Thailand and filmed our interiors at Universal studios. For most of the picture Marlon and I got on extremely well, we kept a good professional relationship. It was tested occasionally.

Marlon, as MacWhite, the new American ambassador to Sarkhan, our fictional Southeast Asian country, is met on arrival at the airport by an immense anti-American riot. He and his wife are caught in their limousine on the tarmac and the screaming crowd tries to turn the limo over and burn it. Their lives are saved by the arrival of government troops. MacWhite has a violent scene with the embassy staff. Late that evening he gets to his residence for the first time. His wife is waiting for him.

We had built a large, beautiful, expensive set of the ambassador's living room. A front door and a foyer led into the large room, all done in teak. Early in the morning I had sketched out the moves I envisioned with the director of photography and he had set the basic lighting. After we rehearsed with the actors, he would do the final focusing.

Marlon arrived more than an hour late. The crew of sixty-three was sitting quietly, there was nothing for them to do. Marlon went into his dressing room to be made up and get into wardrobe. That took another forty-five minutes. The set was tense. If the full crew is doing nothing but waiting, a financial hemorrhage is occurring. Marlon came out to the set, not in a good mood.

I showed him the blocking I had in mind—his wife would greet him at the front door, then they'd cross the foyer and go down into the living room. There they'd play the scene. Marlon watched, then said, "I don't think I'd do that." Your blood goes cold, you've already lost two hours, now . . . what?

"I wouldn't go into the living room. I've been frightened to death by that mob, I'm scared for my country because of the ineptitude of the embassy staff—I think I'd just sit down in the first chair I came to."

He's set the first trap. He knows the set was expensive to build.

"You want to shoot the scene there because you built a set for it? We have to shoot it where it's right for it to be played. I wouldn't go into the fucking living room, someplace comfortable is the last place I'd want to be."

I think Marlon knew the scene would play better in the living room because the plan had been to shoot there—the furniture, the decor, the props, the room to move were there to work with—for Marlon, for me, for the cameraman. But where the scene should be played wasn't the issue. The issue was Marlon didn't want any surly looks or fingers pointed because he'd been late and didn't know his lines. Therefore he created a conflict where authority would be on the defensive.

Where Marlon suggested he sit—just inside the front door—there was no set, only a single painted flat and a prop chair. There was no "wild wall" that could be taken out to shoot reverse angles. And there was no place for his wife to sit.

In a matter of seconds Marlon had created a perfect dilemma for me. Two hours of the shooting day had gone by. To keep from losing more time, I might say all right, I'll shoot the scene in the foyer. But it wouldn't save time because all the lighting would have to be changed. And if I simply accommodated Marlon's approach, the crew might sympathize with my predicament but they'd withdraw their respect.

Sometimes it's impossible to tell whether Marlon's arguing because he cares or because he wants disruption. In this case I think he wanted the day's log to show that shooting was delayed because the director had blocked the scene before discussing it with the star, not because the star was an hour and a half late.

He was the franchise. So I had to accommodate his feelings. Ultimately, we found a compromise. I shot the beginning of the scene in the foyer and the rest in the living room.

There were encounters like this, but most of the time Marlon came to the set ready and worked hard. When he is using all his resources, he is formidable. He knows exactly where his key light is, when he's in or out of it, what lens is on the camera, where the bottom of the frame is, he is expert at matching his actions in all angles. In these times he is the consummate film actor; not only has he prodigious creative talent but full command of the technology of movie production.

His way of working is visceral. A major scene called for him to be extremely angry. We shot it a couple of times, but the real violence wasn't in him. I described in different ways what I thought was called for. He'd say, "I know what you want, I'm just having trouble doing it." After the fourth try he said, "Get away from logic, give me an image."

I knew what he meant, I thought about it for a minute. The year before, Christian, Marlon's son, had been missing for some days and was found in Mexico in the company of a group of hippies. It was alleged that Anna had arranged the kidnapping. I said to Marlon, "Anna's having Christian kidnapped again, those hippies will take him down to that crap hole in Mexico, he'll be scared to death and living in filth."

The rage swelled inside Marlon, his anger roared. "Let's go," he said. We did the scene once more and it was a print.

One night after work we were having a drink in Marlon's dressing room and he suggested we go out and have dinner.

"I'm going to have dinner with a friend of mine from college, Dick Jones, him and his wife," I said.

"Where?"

"At their house in Pasadena."

"What kind of people are they?"

"Dick is chairman of Mitchum, Jones and Templeton, a stock-brokerage firm. Dick's wife, Cynthia, is an absolute beauty, so is her sister, Ann Dudley, she'll be there, too. Pasadena is the epicenter of conservatism, it's a long way from the movie business, Mar."

"Why would you hang out with people like that, what kind of friendship do you have with him?"

"During the war, when I was in naval officer training at UCLA, I became friends with guys from all over the country. Dick has remained one of my closest. Think you'd like to come with me?"

We'd drunk a couple of Scotches during the conversation and it seemed like another interesting frontier. Marlon decided he wanted to come.

At the Joneses', things were convivial and good-natured. People are flattered at Marlon's patient interest in what they do. I was proud of Marlon's good manners, happy with the warmth the Joneses extended, it was a lovely evening. We were finishing the entrée when Marlon turned to Cynthia.

"What size are your moons?" he asked.

"What?"

She'd heard what he said, but it wasn't possible he'd said what she heard.

"The brown areas around your nipples, what are they, about silver-dollar size?" He held up a circle with thumb and forefinger as he munched. She flushed. Marlon waited, pleasant.

"Let's see them," he said.

Maximum disarray in the room. If Marlon continued, just

because of the way he could instantly change the mood to the bizarre, there was a chance Cynthia would actually show her moons. She'd been shocked by his directness and effrontery, she was also on fire. Her eyes were locked to his, her color high. Everybody wanted it to happen and was frightened that it might.

I thought I should slow things down, so I joked she shouldn't show us her moons without a saxophonist playing stripper music. Marlon didn't persist, but he'd gotten the animals moving around—every one at that table had a mental picture of something he'd have said was preposterous only a moment before.

Near the end of filming, things started to fray between Marlon and me. The studio was pleased with the work we'd done and they and Marlon agreed I should direct the comedy he was to do next. We'd almost completed *The Ugly American* when he became removed and uncommunicative.

We were shooting the one emotional scene left. Marlon seemed to be walking through it, there was no fire in him. I talked with him about his energy, we didn't disagree about interpretation because I didn't know what his interpretation was. After each take I urged him to get into it, the scene was crucial. His look was hostile, as if just staying in the room with the tripe he was hearing was sickening. Marlon Brando can act, and when he's showing you what an asshole you are for your interpretation of the scene, for not being aware of your abysmal lack of talent, it's got real punch.

We shot the scene twenty-seven times by actual count. His nearly inert performance didn't vary. I printed the twenty-seventh take and didn't mask my disgust with the way he'd performed.

Just before the picture ended, Marlon said he thought we shouldn't work together on the next picture, things had gotten too strained. I said okay. It was obvious by then that it wasn't possible. But we didn't talk about why, we didn't try to fix it. Time would heal things, but we didn't know that then.

As I look back, some of the friction probably came because I was the authority figure on the set, just my being in charge, and even though Marlon was a lot responsible for my having the position, it made him put on his war paint.

When I was an actor in New York, I once went to read for a road company of the play *Mr. Roberts*. Josh Logan directed the play and was in the theater for the readings. It was a cattle call, every young actor in New York read for Logan. He was at one of the first screenings of *The Ugly American*. I don't think I'd seen him since the day in New York when I read for him, but he came over as if we were old colleagues and said how much he liked the picture. But he was on fire about something else.

"How did you get Marlon to behave, George, he gave a performance, it was a professional piece of work. Directing him in *Sayonara* was a nightmare, he was sullen and silent and acted as if everything about me was offensive, most of all my ideas about directing the picture."

I could imagine what hell it would be to have Marlon behaving that way through a whole picture. Marlon has great power. And great cunning. He uses them often against directors—indeed, against anyone he feels deserves it.

The making of *The Ugly American* was a farrago of my

relationship with Marlon. There were times of fellowship, fun, and laughter, and other times when we were like two kangaroos in a ring with boxing gloves on. There were free and soaring hours uninhibited by anything bad, just two fellows happy to be friends.

7

—

I am not sleeping. This is not a night for sleep, I am in the demesne of the past and more images spool out. As they play on me under the light of a February moon, I overlay a picture of Marlon in bed in the main house trying not to cough, and I wonder again how ill he is. We've talked about how each of us would feel if the other died first. We've tried to imagine it, to take a serious and sober view, but we couldn't stay serious, we made jokes about it. I can't think of any jokes now.

Out on the auto court Sonny and Franny start to bark. Nothing unusual about that, their barking will erupt three or four times a night, but this time their sounds trigger a memory of another night when the dogs, two different ones then, were barking.

———

I had pulled into the parking area below Marlon's house on Mulholland Drive after passing through the tall wrought-iron security gate. Marlon's driveway is long, and at about two hundred yards in, it splits, one branch goes down the hill to Jack Nicholson's house, the other goes up the hill to Marlon's. Marlon's house sits on a crown and has a spreading view, San Fernando Valley to the north, Beverly Hills to the south.

As I stopped, my headlights lit the sign facing me.

WARNING—GUARD DOGS
DON'T LEAVE CAR
HONK HORN UNTIL SOMEONE
COMES TO ESCORT YOU

I opened the door and got out. The dogs, one a rottweiler, the other half German shepherd half wolf, cruised over and bumped my thighs; they knew me. But their fretting and tail switching said they wanted an intruder, someone they didn't know, on whom they could demonstrate their skills. Housed in them was real ferocity, Marlon was in earnest about his privacy.

The rottweiler was scary, huge with hostile eyes. Though the two dogs came up to me together, they were not friends, there was a palpable sense that at some point they would sort out who was top dog.

Three weeks later they did. The battle was hideous and brief. Marlon had been sleeping, but the awful noise pulled him out of bed. He ran to his bedroom door and peered up the hall. After a few moments the rottweiler appeared at the other end. He padded toward Marlon and went past him into the bedroom and lay down. His black coat glistened with flecks of fresh, dark blood. In a back room Marlon found the wolf-shepherd, inert, on his side, his jaw hanging loosely, barely connected to his head.

Periodically, Marlon wants to be alone. "Don't come back till I call you," he tells the secretaries and housekeepers, and shoos them out of the house. This drizzly night was one of those times; Marlon was the only one there.

I followed the flagstones across the lawn and went in through the back door. I passed through the kitchen, went through the swinging door into the dining room, then crossed to the hallway.

I walked down the teak-floored hall to Marlon's bedroom. As I approached, he called from the darkness, "Come in, Georgie, I want you to see something."

The single source of light in the room was a battery-powered black-and-white TV set. Marlon was lying on his back on his bed, the TV atop the mound of his stomach. Shadows from the set, wide, narrow, wide, jumped on his face.

"Jesus, Mar, why the Boris Karloff lighting?"

Marlon pointed to the screen, "Look at this guy, he murdered two people."

I got on the bed where I could see. Marlon was watching *On the Waterfront*. Lee J. Cobb, the tough union leader, was shouting orders to his longshoremen on a raw day on the New Jersey docks. Marlon pointed to one of the men in the near foreground.

"This guy was a hood, too." He tapped the face of another man. "This guy called me Maloo. I don't know if he couldn't say Marlon or just didn't give a shit. 'Hey, Maloo, you talk like us, shoulda been born a wop, Maloo.' He'd pinch my cheek with the knuckles of his second and third fingers."

He paused and we watched in silence. The little screen seemed to intensify rather than take away from the drama. But the real show was Marlon's recall of that time. There he was in the foreground, young, virile, the boxer Terry Malone, who would be betrayed by his brother. Marlon's acting technique was spellbinding, always letting you know there were other things in his head than just the words he was saying. The performance foretold of the career ahead.

Tonight, as he lay looking back on himself, there was no emotion in him, only his absorption with the details of the times he was recalling. We'd said we've have dinner at eight, but he was in no rush to leave, schedules don't interest him. That's why he liked the story of the Alaska fishermen.

Starkist Tuna wanted to make a deal with the Eskimos to buy their catch. Both sides finally agreed on the pay, but when Starkist said the working hours would be nine to five, the Eskimo chief said no.

It was a serious moment, the understanding had taken a long time to work out.

"Why won't you work from nine to five?" asked the lawyer. "That's when everybody else works."

"You pay us to catch fish, is that what you want?"

"Exactly."

"We catch fish when fish come, fish don't know about nine-to-five."

Marlon pointed to a heavyset balding man. "You know how in Tibet they've got prayer wheels along the trails and the Buddhists stop and spin them to make merit?" he said.

"Yes."

"This guy thought you made merit by saying 'fuck.' Every third word was *fuck*. 'Marlon, ya fuck, foist time I fuckin' seen ya without fuckin' makeup . . . fuckin' Sam Spiegel oughta be iced, he fuckin' calls these sandwiches fuckin' lunch.' Sam Spiegel, the producer of the picture, was so cheap he had sandwiches brought to the set instead of hiring a caterer. He didn't know how close he came to being iced," Marlon said. We watched the film continue.

"That guy there—fought in Madison Square Garden for the heavyweight title. He had a funny high-pitched voice that didn't go with that big body."

Marlon's voice became an eerie Irish tenor. "I see these bums fighting today, it's criminal, Marlon, I could beat 'em. I'm forty-one and I think about getting back in shape because when I look at them I'm looking at creeps who don't train, Marlon, bums. I wanna get back in shape, think I could do that? Marlon, I'd like to know what you think."

Like Picasso laying five lines on a sketch pad, Marlon created quick, deft portraits. A few head movements, half gestures, a change of timbre in his voice, and there the longshoreman stood in front of us.

"Had a huge fight with Kazan over this scene," he said. "If I'd done it the way he wanted my whole character wouldn't have made sense." It was one of the most famous scenes in movie history. Marlon and his brother, Rod Steiger, are in the backseat of a limousine and the brother threatens him with a gun.

Elia Kazan was the emperor of the New York theater in those days. He had directed Marlon in *A Streetcar Named Desire*. To disagree with Kazan would take balls enough, but to dictate to him how the scene should be played was awesome stuff.

Marlon put the TV set down on the bed. "Let's go eat," he said. He went to the closet and took out a dark blue velour top. He pulled it over his head, it didn't reach the top of his pants, Marlon was fat.

"We'll go to Valentino, you like Valentino," he said.

"No, let's go somewhere *you'd* like," I replied.

"No, Valentino is okay," said Marlon.

He was putting on cologne. He handed me the bottle. Monsieur, by Givenchy, a scent we both liked. In our earliest days we'd found we used many of the same colognes—Monsieur, Eau de Sèvres, even Chanel No. 5, a woman's cologne.

I needled him about the insinuation that I wanted to go to Valentino because there was something in it for me, even just the cachet of being seen with him, something.

"Mar, this inference that I'll get something out of it if we go to Valentino is stupid."

"You will, you're a prick and an opportunist, it sticks out all over you. I'd trust you with my life, come on, let's go."

I drove. He pushed the seat back as far as it would go then tilted it, he needed the room.

At Valentino, on Pico Boulevard in West L.A., we were greeted by Piero Selvaggio, the owner, an ebullient, tasteful man. His kitchen is one of the finest in the city and he has probably the city's best wine cellar. The restaurant is more Milanese than Roman, a little formal and without the southern Italian floridness. As he led us to our table, the change in the body postures of the diners was subtle but unmistakable. Brando makes an impression.

As we approached the banquette, two busboys pulled the

table out so Marlon would not have a problem getting his stomach by it. He got on the banquette all right but the velour top slipped up and a bravura band of belly presented itself.

"A little bruschetta to start, Marlon?" Piero asked.

"No, no bread, thank you. You have any bamboo shoots, wheat hearts, lemongrass?" Marlon weighed over three hundred pounds but was suggesting he'd like the meal of a Tibetan ascetic.

Piero shook his head and laughed. "Marlon, it's an Italian restaurant, have something we do best, homemade ravioli tonight con funghi, broccoli . . ." His hands flowed expressively. "You know the law says you are not allowed to leave an Italian restaurant without eating some pasta."

"No pasta, thanks, Piero." The world-weary smile: others may suck down those noodles, but for me the exquisite pain of denial.

"Osso bucco, very beautiful also—half order?"

"No, no," Marlon says, the retiree from the world of the flesh. "I'll have the salmon, poached, and a mixed green salad with lemon juice on the side."

"For me, the ravioli, Piero, it sounds delicious, and a little insalata mista," I say.

Piero has had the captain bring over a bottle of red wine.

"Wine, Marlon?"

The patient head move, side to side, no.

"Too bad," says Piero. "This is truly beautiful, Riserva Ducale Speciale, only a few thousand bottles were produced." He pours some in my glass, waits for me to taste. It's superb.

"Perfect, Piero."

"Enjoy, Giorgio."

The entrées arrive. Marlon's salmon is simply done with

two small vegetables alongside, not the meal for which one comes to Valentino. My ravioli, hot, beautifully arranged on the plate, is an invitation. I sail into it. After three or four bites it's time to start working Marlon over. I turn to him.

"Taste?"

"That?"

"Yeah."

"God no."

"This goes in the pasta hall of fame, Mar."

"Been on the diet for five days, can't."

But I've got the hook in him. We talk on for a few minutes, then with no break in the conversation he picks up his fork and impales three of my ravioli and lifts them into his mouth. We keep talking as if nothing unusual has occurred.

Now the Tibetan ascetic has fled and Henry VIII stands in his place. Marlon leans over and grabs my wineglass and downs the contents. "Great. Piero knows his shit."

He beckons to the captain, who steps to the table.

"Mr. Brando?"

Marlon points to the pasta, then makes a circling motion with his fork, another round.

"The same, an order of the pasta for you and another one for Mr. Englund."

"Same for Mr. Englund, bigger for me."

"Right away." He hurries to the kitchen.

Marlon finishes off both his large pasta and my normal one. And my salad. And a plate of Italian bread.

"Dessert?" the captain asks.

"He'll have vanilla ice cream, double," Marlon says.

"*Benissimo*. And for you, Mr. Brando, some tiramisu or we have a homemade fruit tart."

"I'll have the same thing he's having."

"Vanilla ice cream for you also."

"Double," Marlon says.

"Double, yes."

"*Benissimo,*" Marlon replies.

I should make a film of Marlon eating ice cream. As with everything else he does, it's original. Start with the pile he gets on the spoon. Then he conveys it to his mouth, a rhino opening. As I start to take a spoonful of mine, he knocks my spoon aside and takes half of what's in my bowl in one bite.

The meal was over. It was a fine dinner and Marlon had enjoyed himself—which in no way meant that next time he suggested Valentino, it wouldn't be with the same insinuation of hidden benefits for me.

That night had something particular attached to it. Maybe it was sharing the familiar ritual with the pasta, maybe it was the sudden awareness of how long we've been friends, over twenty years, maybe it was the sense we were getting older. But that night was the first time I hugged Marlon.

Back at his house we talked for another couple of hours. I'd said good night and was walking to my car, he was watching me go. I stopped and went back. " 'Night, Mar." I put my arms around him and kissed him on the cheek. He was dear to me, and like a blind man, I wanted to know him by touch. He's huge, I had to shift to encircle him.

It must have been a long season since Marlon had been embraced, no girl could get her arms around him. It's one thing to know that he's huge, it's another actually to pull that immensity to you. He kissed my cheek, " 'Night, Georgie." We held each other a moment, it was natural after all those years.

My mind comes out of the past and back to Brando's star-studded *Master Class* on acting. That DVD must get finished, I think to myself, it must come to life. Because of Marlon's failing health, a sense of urgency now surrounded it. I had written an overview of the project.

> Marlon Brando is the acting colossus of the twentieth century. Others in the century (the most likely candidate being Lord Olivier) gained mastery over the traditional components of acting—elocution, diction, body movement, makeup—to achieve their eminence. But Marlon came like a tornado into the acting house, tore up its furniture, shredded its rule book, smashed its conventions—and an army of imitators formed up behind him.
>
> Marlon brought emotional nakedness to acting. He brought violence. And, as in *A Streetcar Named Desire* and *On the Waterfront,* he wove into the violence an almost alarming tenderness. Marlon revolutionized acting, yet nowhere have we had a comprehensive picture of this outsider who brought to us such inside knowledge of the human soul.
>
> Some scenes from Marlon's movies are among the best ever put on film. In *Master Class,* we will provide tales never revealed before about their origins. With clips from *Streetcar, Waterfront, The Godfather,* etc., Marlon will tell how he came to act the scenes the way he did.

I wrestle awhile, thinking about the best way to move this project forward. I had directed Marlon in *The Ugly American,* I knew his acting capacities firsthand. I knew more than that, I knew how his acting started.

Marlon was pained by his alcoholic mother and belligerent father in his childhood years. Worse was their absences. His father was a traveling salesman and his mother was removed from him by alcohol, falling in and out of awareness during the day. To awaken her when she was intoxicated and slumped in a corner, her son learned to use his performing talents. He would strike poses, imitate their friends, their dogs, horses, and other farm animals, he would act—and she would come to some smiling awareness of him.

Acting has repugnant aspects for him because it recalls anguished childhood days when it was his only means of holding his mother's gaze.

Marlon's performances aren't limited to stage and film. He will give as much attention to some human scene as to a movie in which he's being paid millions to act. He'll devote unlimited time to the seemingly mundane—he'll talk with the drug addict he's just met or the woman who's come to interview him, or his maid. He's not certain at the start what treasure he'll find, but digging and patience will lead to something.

Why does he spend so much time on these excursions? It is from here that the miracle of his acting comes. His performances are made of booty retrieved on these missions inside human souls. Directors he works with know how to make a film. They have experience, sometimes long experience, in the industry. But Marlon has spent his time in the cancerous meat of life, in the room where a brain was dissolving, in the agoraphobic corners, the cavity of fear where so much of the time we live. He doesn't learn lines, he brings back a living heart and shows it to you squeezing in the basin.

He starts not with the words he will speak but with a rag,

a bone, a hank of hair, a thimble, a six-shooter, a shawl . . .
he'll put it around his head, become an old woman sitting in
an Arab souk. The line of his performance will develop from
there. His role may become only a tangent to the story that's
been written, that doesn't matter, he'll do it anyway. The
result will be riveting.

Marlon's acting genius is to me most visible in his improvisations. He describes an incident with Kenji, his Japanese
gardener, an older man, small and lean. Kenji is deeply upset
this day because Toto, the mastiff, and Tim, the rottweiler,
both got out the gate and ran down Mulholland Drive.
They're huge dogs and are never let off the premises. They're
not properly Kenji's responsibility, but he wants Marlon to
know how hard he tried to herd them back in. They're still
out on Mulholland Drive, they wouldn't come in.

Marlon shows Kenji's confusion and perplexity. He gets
inside this Japanese elder who has been in this country for
forty years but never learned to speak the language. Trying to
explain about the dogs is forcing him to use more English
than he possesses. He searches through the henhouse of his
English words, embarrassed by his inadequacy, his loss of
face. A Japanese phrase comes out, nasal, sopranic, then a
moan, a long inhale. Marlon has done them exquisitely, his
picture of this dejected old man is like a Zen garden, simple,
only a few lines to fix its life.

In February 1958, Marlon was one of five nominated by
the Academy of Motion Picture Arts and Sciences as Best
Actor for 1957 for his performance in *Sayonara*. There was
the usual publicity across the country and hot conjecture
about what picture and which actors would win.

When Marlon was nominated for *On the Waterfront* there

was little question that he would win. With *Sayonara* there was real doubt. Marlon seemed to be bothered more than excited by the nomination. He dislikes awards ceremonies, he thinks they're mean-spirited, inaccurate, hurtful. He says the only way you can say one performance is better than another is if all competitors have played the same role. Certain scenes in one actor's work might be excellent, aspects of another performance might be outstanding in a different way. Why not leave it at that, why invoke an artificial standard that declares one performance best?

Marlon did not associate excellence with *Sayonara*. He was contemptuous of Josh Logan, the director, and from the beginning, Marlon hadn't liked the script. Immediately after agreeing to do the picture, he began to rewrite it and asked me to work on it with him. I did.

But even though Marlon was not proud of *Sayonara*, he now had his own company. His presence at the Oscars, let alone winning one, would add to Pennebaker's prestige and give the company more weight in the industry. Senior; Jay Kanter, Marlon's agent; Alice, his secretary; everyone urged Marlon to go. But Marlon couldn't connect to the idea, he was in New York and hadn't even decided if he'd come back in time.

Marlon called me from New York and asked if I would go with him if he decided to attend. I said I would. That didn't decide him either. We talked more, he said the Academy Awards weren't important, it didn't matter if he went or not. But the issue was on his mind and a decision wasn't coming easily.

I don't think it had occurred to Marlon at that time to accept the award in absentia or have someone else accept it as he did when he won for *The Godfather*. Two years ago he told me the Academy called and said they wanted to give him their Lifetime Achievement Award, would he attend the ceremony? He said he would not attend. They said in that case they would not make the award. Marlon thought it was curious that his life's work merited the award, but whether or not they bestowed it depended only on whether he'd attend the ceremony.

I thought about why Marlon was in conflict, why he didn't want to go to the Academy Awards. It seemed he felt that to go was to lend himself to *them,* their system of excellence, their description of the best. Marlon had pledged a long time ago not to be part of them, he was different from them, outside their city.

Marlon's sense of being an outsider began in his earliest years. He loved the animals on the farm in Nebraska where he grew up and he loved Ermi, the black woman who took care of him. He thinks that his attraction to dark-skinned women comes from the comfort of being physically close to Ermi. He describes so well the serenity and bliss of being next to her in bed. Once, while he was telling me about Ermi, I asked what had become of her.

"Mar, did you ever see Ermi after you left home?"

"When I was doing *Streetcar* in New York, she came backstage once."

"What was that like, was it emotional?"

"She wanted to borrow money."

He said it matter-of-factly, but after the many times, the many ways he'd described his feelings for Ermi, there had to be some ball of fire connected to that meeting in his dressing room.

"Was that all?"

"Pretty much."

"That must have been sad, Mar. You'd loved her all these years, and instead of being the affectionate woman you'd kept in your thoughts, she just came and asked for money."

Marlon seemed to want the memory to stay distant; he shrugged. "That's life," he said. "She needed money."

Of all the personal revelations Marlon and I have shared, this one is among the saddest. And we'd never talked about it. It would have been unkind to badger him more about something he didn't want to think about, so I didn't. It's a heartbreaking picture to me, I think that visit from Ermi must have given support to his feeling that no woman would be constant.

The day before the awards Marlon was still in a quandary, so we worked out a contingency plan. He would fly to Los Angeles and arrive about an hour before the ceremony started. I'd pick him up at the airport dressed in my dinner jacket and have his tux with me. If he decided to go, he could change in the car and we'd head to the Pantages Theatre. If he decided not to go, we'd drive to Beverly Hills and have dinner. I went to his house and Alice and I collected his tux and all the gear.

First off the plane was Patty Wellman, director Bill Wellman's pretty daughter, who was a flight attendant with TWA. Marlon and I knew her from having flown to New York with her often. He came out next and gave her a showy kiss for my benefit. The three of us shot the breeze awhile; I could see Marlon hadn't made a decision.

"I just heard on the car radio that the Academy Awards are tonight, Mar," I said. "Got any interest in going?"

"Can you believe it, he still hasn't decided, he's crazy," Patty chimed in.

"What do you think I should do?" Marlon said to her.

"Go. For God's sake, you're up for Best Actor, get moving. I'm going home to watch you on TV. Are you guys going or not?"

"Good luck tonight, Mr. Brando," an army sergeant said quietly as he passed. "Enjoyed being on the flight with you." His wife, pink and flushed from having been so close to Marlon, smiled. Marlon waved back.

Patty looked at her watch. "Forget it, he hasn't even got the right clothes on. I'm not going to worry about it, you're both insane."

"Got my stuff?" Marlon said.

"In the car," I said.

We left.

As we came out of the airport, I started moving quickly through the traffic; there wasn't much time.

"Why don't you put on your dinner jacket," I suggested.

"I'm still not sure I want to go."

"I know, but if you put it on, you have all the choices. You can look at the theater, and if you want to go in, I'll park. If you don't, I lay a little rubber and we're gone."

He started taking off his shoes. "I really have reservations," he said.

"Maybe you're making it too much of a philosophical problem."

"That's what it is, though, you do things or you don't do them based on what you believe."

"Sure, but deciding whether to go or not go to the Academy Awards doesn't constitute a moral crisis—these people who are up for awards are thinking how fast they'll fire their publicists if they don't win."

"That's right, it's about publicity, taking ads in *Variety* to get votes, then taking out more ads to thank everybody for giving you the votes you asked for. Some measure of excellence. I don't want to be part of that—the winner, the losers, all that crap."

"I think most people feel the point is to give value to the work we do, to say we all try every year, this year this is the work that succeeded best."

Marlon's shirt was off, he was getting out of his pants.

"That's you saying it, I didn't hear it from anyone in the Academy. Fuck it, it has nothing to do with me . . . I'm a coyote on the outskirts of town, lying down by the side of the road, tired, tongue in the dirt, get up, run again. I look into towns from the outside. You're an outsider, too, but in a different way. Are we the only two who see things the way we do?"

"Somebody else," I said. "Did you ever read *Caligula,* the play by Albert Camus?"

"No, never read it."

"Caligula is the young, moody, Roman emperor, he frightens his counselors."

"Was his last name Brando?"

"Could have been. His sister dies and he is destroyed, there is talk he had been incestuous with her. He goes to her funeral then disappears, no one's seen him in three days. The counselors are nervous, where is he, what's he going to do next? In the early morning Caligula suddenly shows up, hair wet, caked with mud. One counselor, Helicon, is in the room. He says good morning to Caligula, Caligula says good morning matter-of-factly, offers no explanation about the way he looks or where he's been. Helicon says you're looking tired.

Caligula says I've walked a lot. And Helicon says, yes, you've been away quite awhile. Caligula sits watching Helicon, it makes Helicon nervous. Caligula says, it was hard to find. Helicon: 'What was hard to find?' Caligula: 'What I was after.' Helicon: 'Meaning?' Caligula: 'One of the things I haven't got. I saw it but I couldn't get it.' Helicon: 'That's too bad.' Caligula: 'Yes, that's why I'm tired.' "

One of Marlon's legs was out of his pants and he had stopped, intent on the story.

"What was he looking for?" Marlon said.

"Helicon asked him, 'What was it you couldn't get, Caligula?' " I leaned forward and pointed up toward the night sky through the windshield. Marlon's face followed, he stretched to see where I was pointing.

"The moon," I said softly. Marlon craned to see the moon. " 'This world of ours, the scheme of things, as they call it, is intolerable,' " Caligula says. " 'That's why I want the moon, or happiness, or eternal life—something that isn't of this world—bring me the moon, Helicon.' " Marlon, entranced, was still looking up to see the moon.

"No, Mar, I was acting. I was being Caligula asking for the moon."

He'd gotten lost, not just in the story but in what Caligula wanted—happiness, eternal life, something not of this world. He sat with one foot in his tux trousers, head lifted to the sky, balls hanging out, looking for the moon.

I was in evening dress, driving fast; Marlon was undressed listening to Caligula's craziness, or truth, and being deeply touched by it. We were silent, then Marlon looked at me and started to laugh. We both laughed, one outsider telling the other outsider about a third outsider who lived two thousand years ago.

When we turned onto Hollywood Boulevard, Marlon was completely dressed and had decided we should go to the awards. The limousines were parked somewhere else, but the crowd was still in the bleachers, they'd stay until the ceremony was over to see the stars again. The valets opened our car doors. Marlon got out, and when he came into view, the squeal went to the sky. Arriving after all the others, he was a grand surprise, the bleachers rocked.

Marlon waved and sauntered across the sidewalk as if this late arrival was all planned so he would get the big response.

As we slid into our seats, the first award was about to be presented. But though we sat in the theater, neither of us was there. We were back in Caligula's palace.

I don't remember what picture won or to whom Marlon lost. I remember Marlon with his pants around his ankles craning to see the moon that Caligula demanded be brought to him. I remember that somewhere between the airport and Hollywood Boulevard, as the curtain was about to rise on the most important event in the entertainment industry's year, Marlon and Caligula and I were lost in a search for something not of this world.

8

—

For any producer, the process of getting Marlon into a picture was circuitous and subject to his many caprices, with a high likelihood of failure. Often Marlon asked me to be with him when he was going to hear a pitch.

"Come for lunch, I'd like you to tell me what you think of this guy," he said one day.

"Who?"

"Italian producer. Wants me to do his script."

"Are you going to do it?"

"He thinks it's all set."

"What makes him think that?"

"He agreed to pay me ten million against ten percent of the gross."

"Going to do it?"

"Maybe. For the money."

"Good script?"

"I haven't read it, scanned a few pages, doesn't look good."

"Well, that's pushy of him, asking you actually to read the script, you should get a million up front just for that."

At one time Marlon's entire house was done in traditional Japanese style, guests removed their shoes on entering. The living room is Americanized now, though with traces of the formal Oriental chamber it once was. Two of the walls are sliding-glass doors that display the wide view of the San Fernando Valley on one side, Beverly Hills and west to the Pacific on the other.

The Italian producer and two assistants—one man, one woman, she in dark clothes and sensible shoes to look businesslike—and Marlon and I are in that living room. It is a big moment in the producer's life, he is all Mediterranean brio, his cologne is at flood status, his laugh is ready for launch.

A handsome lunch has been brought up from a French restaurant. Marlon doesn't rush to business talk, he remarks on the view out the window, splendid and clear today. He talks about Bob Balzer, from whom he bought the house.

The Italian producer likes the view, he likes what Marlon likes.

Marlon's shit detector starts clicking.

"How long you have lived here, Marlon?" says the producer.

"George, you remember how long?"

"Years, Mar, I think since 1960."

"*Spettacolo.*" The producer gestures to the outside, then turns to his colleagues. They nod in appreciation of this magnificent aerie. "In Italy you don't found such a place, Marlon."

Marlon has the Italian in his crosshairs, he will extract a price for the man's ersatz enthusiasm.

"How's the Beverly Hills Hotel," Marlon says, "meet any good-looking girls?"

The producer laughs the way Italians do when the subject of women comes up.

"In the hotel are pretty girls everywhere around, but pretty girls we find also in Rome, Marlon. This visit is for only meeting with you."

"Been to the Polo Lounge?"

"Of course, yes, who can avoid?"

"Around five-thirty the bar fills up with pretty girls. You like black girls, Carlo?"

"No, for me, is no my taste, anyway, I don't care so much what color is somebody. Yes, eh, no, is yes, many girls."

"I met this black girl in Harlem, her name was Cary, I always wanted to know where she got that name," Marlon says.

The Italians wear the look of the privileged, Brando is going to share something personal with them.

"A party at a nightclub uptown, everybody was black except me and two others. I saw her and went over and started talking. Her eyes were black marbles, simply beautiful. And her tits weren't just high, they were aimed at you."

Marlon surveys to make sure he's getting the marvel of this girl across. There's a shadow of concern on the producer's face, a black girl's tits, *che fai*, what does this portend?

"She knew she had great tits, she'd watch you looking at them, rock her head with her eyes on you, that's right, I know what's happenin' downstairs with your dick."

Downstairs with your dick? The producer is startled, the smiles of the others are kept in place by muscle, not mirth.

"She wasn't educated but could she talk. And when the fucking started, lawdy, she was Edna St. Vincent Millay."

The word *fucking* lands like a cod on the producer's lap. The European good manners he brought are in tatters. Marlon imitates the sensual Cary, pantomimes her sitting on his lap facing him during sex.

"Big boy, what you doin', you fuckin' Cary?" He's both hilarious and mesmerizing.

"You got that right, baby." Marlon has her buttocks in his hands.

"How long you gonna fuck Cary good like that?"

"About a week."

Marlon imitates her burst of laughter, loud and free.

The Italian producer is a pilgrim in an El Greco painting. He came to hear Brando's thoughts on the script and Brando is telling about fucking with a black girl here in the living room with the nice lunch all around, *Dio,* what will come next?

Plenty.

"The way she flexed her buttocks was learned in some erotic Valhalla," Marlon continues, "but when you'd start to come, it was her voice, her voice absolutely melted your balls."

"Eh," from the producer.

Marlon is full of passion and seduction as Cary. "We comin' home now, darlin, give them babies to Cary, that's right, she wants them babies."

Marlon is happy in his recall. Maybe one of you has a fucking story you'd like to share, be glad to hear it. His smile is an invitation.

Breathy fragments from the other two Italians.

"*Alora.*"

"*Fascinato.*"

The producer is in a small boat clinging to the gunwales. Exactly where Marlon wants him.

One of the most telling aspects of Marlon's acting is the way he uses objects. He is magnetic now as he reaches to the table, lifts the script, and sets it on his lap. He presses on it, his hands moving outward from the center as if to smooth out the wrinkles. What else this ritual means you don't know, all you know is you can't take your eyes away. He turns the script ninety degrees toward him, he can now see the corners of the pages he's turned down.

"Let's talk about the script," he says.

The producer gestures. "No, we are anxious to hear, please."

Marlon waits for stillness as well as silence. He begins with the script's positive aspects. They are not many in his view, they do not take long to list. Then he looks to the negatives. He finds the script, he says—the Italians lean forward—spirit-less, desultory.

Spiritless? Desultory? The producer turns to the assistants and blurts in Italian, "I have the contracts in my briefcase, I want to sign the deal and leave, what is going on?"

"The script tries to be something dramatic," Marlon says, "but the role is impossible to perform, it's basically a piece of shit."

The Italian bounces. A piece of shit? He yodels at the aides. "Filming begins in three weeks, I signed a pay-or-play contract with the director, I paid for the studio space, sets are already built, who made this meeting? *Stronzi*"—you shits—"I want to know who made this meeting?!"

He gyrates to me, what do I have to do with this?

Marlon, unperturbed, starts to tell what he might have done if the role had something to play, if it explored some aspect of human behavior, had mischief, magic, or menace in it. He begins to improvise, he is insinuating, he is declamatory, he is hooded, he is sly, he is sexual. He's Billy the Kid shooting quarters off your hat, Pavarotti ripping off a high C then tapering it to a whisper. For some unaccountable reason Marlon selects this moment to display the very best of his acting genius.

"Bravo, Brando!" the producer wants to scream, he wants to leap to his feet and lead the applause for this fantastic performance. But Brando has used his acting riches to tell how awful the script is. When Marlon finishes, the script is back on the table. No longer a blueprint for a movie about to be produced, it is a lifeless prop. Brando will not be appearing in this film.

The producer blinks slowly. Life was going to be incredible. He'd have been a big man in Rome for twenty years, he would have produced a Brando picture. A shrug works through him. "Eh, beh," he says softly.

But there's more to it. In part of the producer there's a lightness, he's had three full hours with Brando, the event of a lifetime . . . *stupendo, enormo, lo fine del mondo!* Wait till he tells them in Rome about the story of the black girl, *ecco!*

The enigma of Marlon. The producer's film has been savaged and that has destroyed the man. Then comes a resurrection, Brando found possibilities in the role so far beyond anything they saw—of course he didn't want to do it.

They're gone. Marlon dissects the meeting. He was affronted by the man's unctuousness and ego.

"Did you see his cheek twitch when I asked what his producer's fee would be?" Marlon asks. He becomes the Italian. "Why you ask such a questions, Marlon, we enjoy ourselves ina you house with the view. Lawyers talk, you and I no discuss the business, *caro*."

The accent and gestures are fine mimicry. Marlon repeats the empty stare he used that said he wanted an answer from the producer.

I take the Italian producer's part. "A percentage of the budget, Marlon. Believe me, I non retire to Capri on fees from this film." I smile to my colleagues, what a joke to think I could steal something for myself. "Heh, heh, heh, no, Marlon, I take a normal fee, *basta*."

We laugh again. There is cruelty in what has transpired. Marlon has been funny, but why didn't he just say, "No thanks, I don't want to be in your picture," why punish the man? I don't say anything. I should have. Instead I've enjoyed it and been a co-conspirator.

The deal is killed. So likely will the next one. Marlon will find the tinny pride in the next producer who gets a big office because he is in charge of a Brando project and Marlon will eviscerate him for it.

I am producing a film called *The Shoes of the Fisherman* in Rome. Anthony Quinn is to star as Kiril Lakota, the man who becomes pope, Laurence Olivier will play the head of the Soviet Union who tortured him for twenty years. Tony and I are both anxious for him to have intimate knowledge of monastic life. I have arranged tonight for us to visit with the Marist priests at their order house to learn about their lives.

I've forgotten why, but Marlon is in Rome, too. I have invited him to be with us and he is eager to come, his curiosity is piqued. He and Tony haven't seen each other since they acted together in *Viva Zapata!,* so when we meet outside the order house, a reunion takes place.

It is to be a hair-down evening, I've talked with the father general, a man from Minnesota, and discussed with him how important it is we get a bare look at the life of priests under the evangelical vows. He says he understands what we want and will try to provide it. During dinner the priests are friendly, but none begins to reveal much that is personal in front of Tony, Marlon, and me, most of all in front of the father general. A discussion of this kind is not the everyday in an Order House.

The Marists work in the Pacific as missionaries. Their lives are spent among Trobriand Islanders and New Guineans. They tell us of this life, of being often in very primitive conditions. Three returned only yesterday from a remote part of New Guinea, four of the others at this table will leave to replace them the day after tomorrow. The message of the Christian God is not left long unsaid in their faraway parish.

The talk is interesting, in fact fascinating, but it is not yet visceral, we have not yet crossed to the insides of these men. The father general is a pleasant moderator, he brings a good story out of one shy priest, encourages another to tell why he took holy orders and why he chose the Marists. The man responds, but what he says is merely informative, not bone and sinew. The father general can see the restraint in these men. He begins to talk about himself. I watch Marlon; he is quiet, listening.

The father general joined the order when he finished college at the University of Minnesota. All his boyhood friends are now presidents and vice presidents of corporations. They have families, children, and grandchildren, and the reassurance that goes with being married and having left something of yourself in the world. He has only his commitment to God. He tries to say exactly what that means. As a priest he must celebrate the mass every day. That time is sacred to him. Without that daily rededication of his life to Christ he would have lost his mind, the doubts that assail him are too terrifying.

He pauses, allowing his most difficult thoughts to come forward. The strain has been awful sometimes, he says quietly. He tries not to feel envious of his friends, but it is a formidable task. To escape from the sense of emptiness, of purposelessness, is often difficult, sometimes not possible. He longs for the children he didn't have and now will never have, he is passionate to hear their voices, to see the need of him in their eyes. He is driven sometimes to the point of distraction with the questions that explode inside him. Has he done the right thing, is there a God? Or has he thrown away his life on a myth? His doubts are alarming, his distress is deep, it is transferred to us. I wonder if the father general will be all right alone tonight because this good man is close to cracking.

Softly, with the intimacy of one soul to another, Marlon asks him a question. "Have you ever crossed the line, ever answered no, there is no God, and wanted to tear the cross from around your neck?"

"Not yet," the father general answers with equal softness. He pauses. "And at this point I doubt I ever will. I am sixty-two and the winds have died down inside me, I am at peace with the place God has found for me in His order.

The room is thawed, the other priests begin to let loose their innermost thoughts. We hear that each of them, every single one of them, has been at some time—and for some of them it has been most of the time—gripped with the same questions: Have I done the right thing in giving my life to God? Is there a God? None of them says he is completely sure there is, yet they have pledged the one life they have to a more perfect understanding of Him. They have agreed to own nothing, to be chaste, to be obedient. Was it wise? Does it even make sense?

I look to Marlon, he is lost in their stories, this is human drama in a form he has never known. He wants to remember and store these men and this night.

The priests' openness about their duties and their doubts makes it an extraordinary evening. Each of them is singular, inquiring, and heroic in his way. But none is so memorable as the father general. He says he hadn't planned to speak, he thought he would moderate the evening, but he's been having these thoughts for a long time and they all came out in this gathering. He hopes it's helped, he's calm, not embarrassed. He sees himself as an instrument of the Almighty and there is no question in his mind that God wanted this evening to go as it has.

There is a shared mood among Tony, Marlon, and me. We have probed and asked questions and we have been brought to consider, in this unusual hall, what it is we truly believe. Is there anyone or anything in our lives for whom we would be able to make such sacrifices?

When we leave, we are different from when we entered this house. We will not have the answers to the big questions tonight, but neither will we ever be completely free of those questions again.

It's late and Tony has to be at the studio early in the morning. He smiles. "Yolanda will never believe I have been out this late talking with Marlon and George and a bunch of priests." We laugh with him and Marlon and I give him an *abbraccio*, a hug. Tony says good night and gets in his car.

Marlon and I decide to walk through the old city. It is late but we are young souls tonight, animated by ancient Rome all around us and by the ancient questions that were raised with the priests. Here, where both Peter and Paul entered the city, where Peter is buried, where the bones of Christian martyrs lie in the Catacombs, we try to get at the eternal mysteries.

I think, as I listen to us, that our views of God come from our views of our fathers.

"The 'Our Father' they talk about in prayers, is really an extension of our earth fathers," I say. "Your father and mine are the reasons neither of us is able to believe in God."

Marlon has no patience with the idea of a divine father who would care for him. Belief in God is infantile, it's mythology, he says.

Yes, it does seem that God has been created in the image of man and not the other way around, I agree. Still, tonight, while we shared our humanity, our fears, was there a presence with us? Something? Someone? Christ said, "For where two or three are gathered together in my name, there am I in the midst of them." Could it have been He who joined us in that little meeting about why we were here and what we are to do while we live?

There is romance as we walk, the romance of touching the great questions together, the romance of simply being us this night, the romance of walking on the special plot of land the ancient Romans called Mediterranea, the center of the earth.

Shadows of its majestic architecture are all around us and with our gestures, our rising and falling voices, our walking backward, our stopping to present another view, we look like any two Romans who have strode these old stones through the hundreds of years. Marlon and I talk on, this is a night to keep in our grasp, we relinquish it only when the stars have given way to the morning.

9

In that guest bedroom up on Mulholland Drive earlier this year, some of those questions haunted me again. Why do we have to die? Why will it soon be over for Marlon and me? Who designed this system where humans are born new and filled with promise—and then are sent to "suffer the thousand natural shocks which flesh is heir to."

I hadn't planned to be in turmoil this night, preoccupied with the eternal questions; it was to be another in the endless string of buoyant times when Marlon and I were together. I hadn't planned that this night would make it clear and certain that our string will not last forever, that our string is now a frayed bit of rope that extends only a small way from my hand. Still, I recall what George Bernard Shaw wrote: "Life is no brief candle to me. It is a sort of splendid torch which I have got hold of for the moment, and I want to make

it burn as brightly as possible before handing it on to future generations."

In the planetary swirl of this night another shard of memory, unattached to anything else, comes forward in my mind.

I'd come up to Marlon's house for lunch. When I arrived I couldn't find him. He wasn't in the kitchen or the living room or the dining room. I finally located him in his bathroom, he was sitting in front of a table he'd brought in with a mirror on it. It seemed a primitive arrangement. When he turned around to greet me his face was distorted, he had stuffed Kleenex or something like it between his lower lip and his teeth.

"I like it, Mar," I said. "I'm tired of seeing you with a normal face, what else are you going to do?"

"They're coming up to do a test."

"Who?"

"Coppola."

"You're going to do a screen test?"

"I guess you could call it that."

"Well, when you're starting out in the business you have to humble yourself and do what you're asked."

"It's going to be informal, see how we both feel."

"Any particular role or is it just to see if you can act."

The Godfather.

I didn't say anything for a long minute. "Mar, what a masterful idea."

Still fiddling with the mass in his chin, he turned to me, surprised. "You think so?"

"You as Don Corleone . . . brilliant."

"Why?"

"First of all what you'll bring to the role, what you've

already started to create. Second it's the world of the Mafia, you in the center of that is magic. Did you read the book?"

"A bit of it, I read more of the screenplay. It seems okay."

"See you're not tuned to the gossip on the rialto. This is the hottest picture going and you in that role is a perfect match."

Marlon was not as excited as I was about his playing the Godfather, but Coppola came up and they did a sort of improvised test and of course what Coppola thought from the first was true, that the role was made for Marlon and Marlon was made for the role.

A couple of nights after Marlon won the Oscar for his performance in *The Godfather*, we were at dinner and he still didn't see what all the excitement was about.

"I've worked harder in other pictures and I think I did a better job in some of them," he said. "*Appaloosa*, for instance, I spent a lot of time on that role, did my best. The picture went nowhere and hardly anything was said about my performance."

We shook our heads about the ironies of life.

Marlon and I both intended to be good fathers. Whatever happened later, we began with high resolve. We wanted to give our children a better deal than we had had. Marlon wanted his children to see someone other than the intimidating Brando Sr. I wanted my children never to doubt their father loved them and was always their defense and support.

Among my children, Marlon had a soft spot for my second son, Bryan. They were kindred rebels. Bryan was the adventurer among our brood, the turbulent one, the explorer looking over the top of the next hill. He might have been an astronaut or a surgeon, a musician, an actor, had his life not been consigned to drugs.

When I was separated from Cloris, my deepest concern was that Bryan was not getting the teaching he needed, learning self-discipline. He needed most to be guided, I saw danger for him if he didn't have a steady hand near. He lived with his mother and my influence was diminished. I think Marlon didn't like what he perceived as my authoritarian way with Bryan—his old sensitivity to his own father's angry authority.

Bryan started on drugs when he was fourteen and that problem became the center of my life. It was a principal subject between Marlon and me, we discussed it often and at length, each new initiative I tried, each new horror that arrived. Once I said, "I can't lose this one." Marlon said, "It's not a war. Give Bryan room, don't think he's going to be this way forever. When it's time for him to quit, he'll quit."

I never took hope from what Marlon said because I knew too much, I was closer to Bryan's drug use than anyone. It *is* a war. If there is any hope of reclaiming a drug user, it's because someone commits all his resources to the cause. The addict ultimately must cure himself, but he first has to get to the point where he can see he has choices. That takes a monumental battle.

When Bryan was sixteen I took him and George Jr. down to Tetiaroa hoping Bryan could clean out there. I was ready to go to Bhutan with him or to an igloo in the Arctic, anything and anywhere to separate him from drugs. But that was something I wanted, he did not. I asked him once if he could imagine a life without drugs, without any reference to drugs. He tried to temper what he said out of deference to me, but the answer was no, he could not.

Bryan did well on Tetiaroa. Christian, a couple of years younger than Bryan, and Miko, a couple of years younger than Christian, were also there, and thcy canoed in the lagoon, fished, and played games on the beach. I allowed myself some hope. That is the most devastating mistake a parent of a child on drugs can make. But you have no choice, you're powerless to change anything, so in spite of what you see and know, you hope. Blindly, unreasonably, you hope for the miracle from above to save your child. And then you are truly doomed, it gets worse.

On Tetiaroa, Marlon proposed to Bryan that he would give him fifty thousand dollars to stop using drugs. If he used drugs of any kind, even beer, he'd lose a third of the money. If he took drugs a second time, he'd lose another third; if he used drugs a third time, the rest of the money would be confiscated. Marlon later recalled the arrangement to someone while I listened.

"Bryan was down in the islands where there wasn't anything I knew of besides booze—and he went through three-thirds of it. Bryan was funny, charming, strong, full of laughter, full of jokes. He was a drummer, I was a drummer, I had a lot invested in Bryan, a part of me was very deeply injured by his death."

In that same conversation Marlon said his technique with his own kids was to let them smoke dope in another room because he'd rather see it under his nose than worry about what was going on out in the valley. Marlon used some prophetic words, he talked of "the impending disasters that have to do with Christian's life."

On a rainy night Marlon and I were sitting in the usual place, near the fireplace in the sitting area of his bedroom. I told him the latest about Bryan.

Bryan was in the L.A. County Jail—again. I said this time I was not going to bail him out unless he agreed to go to an inpatient clinic for treatment. He finally agreed. I picked him up that night. It is no treat to drive into downtown L.A. after 10 P.M., park, and retrieve your son from the interior of the county jail. I took him home, we talked for a while, then went to sleep. Bryan came with me to the studio the next morning. I had tried all day the day before to find a good place for Bryan, but I hadn't succeeded. Time was desperately important; if he left my sight, he'd have something in him in an hour.

I called all over the United States, to places in Massachusetts, Florida, Connecticut. None could take him in on such short notice, others did not seem interested. I called the famous Hazelden facility, in Minnesota. They needed medical reports and a biography before they would discuss admission. I didn't find out till years later that my father had been a founder of Hazelden. If I'd known, maybe that "credential"—that Bryan was Rip's grandson—would have gotten him in.

Late in the afternoon, my despair growing, I called a place in Venice, California, called Tuum Est. I'd heard there was a good director there, a black man named Eddie. When I began telling him my story, he said, "Mr. Englund, it's after five o'clock and we close at five, I'm on my way home." I asked if there was any way he could wait for me, I'd come now. He must have heard the anguish in my voice, something made him say, "Come on over, I'll wait."

It's an old brick building right on the boardwalk in Venice. Eddie's office on the second floor looks out over the Pacific. He is lean and energetic, in his late thirties. Polite but no civilities, his is street etiquette. He told me he was an ex–heroin addict and had served seven years in the Washington State Penitentiary for murder. He listened while I told Bryan's story, the history of drug use and all that went with it, the lying, the stealing, the fighting. Bryan and I had two physical fights, one when a dealer came up to Cloris's house and I was there. The second time, under the influence of drugs, he was swearing at me, baiting me—"Fuck you, what are you going to do about it?" I wasn't offended by the language, it's seeing your child in that condition, something deep and helpless comes up inside you. I told Eddie I'd used up my thoughts, my care, and my tears, I was in need of help myself.

Bryan didn't stay at Tuum Est, but I did. I went back several times to talk with those living there. Maybe thirty or forty of them, men and women, they'd ask me questions about anything. "You in the movie business, how many movie stars you fuck?" It wasn't a funny question, it was a real question. Everything there was real. When you've lost everything from drugs and all that's left is your life and that's about to go, too, everything is real, especially your fear.

Marlon wanted to meet Eddie. He and Cloris and I all went down there for a session with Eddie and his partner, another ex–heroin addict with a blond mustache who looked like a member of the Royal Canadian Air Force. It was to be a no-holds-barred talk about us and our kids and drugs, Tuum Est style.

It was useful to Cloris and Marlon. There was little in it for me because I already knew what I needed to know and no enlightenment was going to help it. Bryan was going to die. And I had a front-row seat for the rest of the story.

Marlon liked Eddie. He had Eddie and his wife up to his house for dinner. Later on he sent them to Tetiaroa for a vacation. He had earnest talks with Eddie. Eddie could not believe that Marlon Brando would call him up, would answer when he called. It was all too much for this man who'd grown up in the ghetto of Oakland, California. What did he have that nobody else had ever seen in him that Marlon Brando saw and made Marlon Brando his friend? Must be something because it was Marlon Brando, for Christ's sake. Shit! Marlon Brando!

So when Marlon started not to answer Eddie's calls, when the glue that held Eddie in Marlon's thoughts let go, well, Eddie had trouble managing that. The central problem for recovering addicts is low self-esteem. And no matter how long it's been since you've had a fix, you're always a recovering addict, you're always working on that self-esteem problem. It's hard to get anything but a bottom job, you've got no résumé, you're in your thirties.

"What have you been doing, Eddie, been on vacation all this time?"

"No, sir, I was in prison for seven years because I murdered a man and I was on heroin for eleven years after that. But I want this job very badly, sir, and I'll work hard if you'll give me the chance."

Bryan's death a year later started two weeks of hell. Marlon was a little uncertain about what to say to me. It's not a war, he had said. But it was and we lost it. I was too grief-stricken to turn to Marlon in anger and say, "See how wrong you were, drugs kill, and it is a war against them." I regretted that I'd listened to Marlon at all about Bryan.

There was a gathering at Cloris's house. Marlon came. He was at his most reserved, as if someone might take advantage of him. Also, it was very difficult to comfort me. His constant advice had been lighten up, people change, Bryan will change, don't get so bent out of shape. His advice was meant to be helpful, but it wasn't thought out. There was no comfort for me that day that Marlon was my friend. He did not come to the service in the church in the Pacific Palisades. I didn't want to go, I didn't want to be there with Bryan's mother, his brothers, his sister, his friends, the mother of his child. I believed they could have and should have done more to save Bryan's life.

Katie Sagal, who had grown up with Bryan, sang "Amazing Grace." It had nothing to do with the truth of Bryan. In a room at the YMCA in New York, he died a dirty disgraceful death from crack. We shouldn't be in a sunny church in Pacific Palisades singing psalms and telling sweet remembrances, we should be called to account.

"You first, you are Bryan Englund's father?"

"Yes, sir."

"Did you understand that from his birth you were responsible for his life?"

"Yes, sir."

"His education, his preparation for adulthood?"

"Yes, sir."

"Do you understand that without mitigating evidence you bear the principal responsibility for your son's death?"

"I know that, yes, sir."

"Do you have any such evidence to present?"

"No, sir, I haven't."

"Very well. You are condemned as follows: Every time you hear music Bryan liked, every time you see his picture, touch his child, you will remember the baby you held in your arms, the careful time you and Cloris took to name him Bryan. A thousand thoughts of Bryan will fall on you, meteorite showers in your nights. There is no possibility of parole, there will be no time off for good behavior, there is no appeal of this sentence."

Since Marlon's son Christian committed murder, Marlon is serving a similar sentence. Not as severe, his son is still alive, but terrible enough.

In the early sixties Marlon and I rented Henry Kaiser's house at Diamond Head in Hawaii for Christmas. We were right on the beach, so the kids had a grand time, but they liked the inside of the huge house best. The floor of the living room was all marble. They took the bar chairs, small barrel backs with casters, and shot across the expanse in an expensive demolition derby.

On New Year's Eve we chartered a yacht and cruised offshore so the kids could watch the fireworks. It was a special time, I think it was one of the most relaxed holidays Marlon and I ever had. The kids—well, all of us—were young and knew how to let go and party.

Georgie remembers going to Tetiaroa ten years later, he remembers snorkling with Christian late one afternoon and losing track of the time. When they finally looked up it was dark and they were way out in the middle of the lagoon. They'd been watching big sharks and now the sharks were still there, but they couldn't see them. They stood on coral heads, afraid and imagining. The longer they stood there and the more they thought, the more frightening their predicament was.

Nobody could see them way out there, nobody knew where they were. But the big sharks knew where they were. The two boys couldn't decide whether to try to swim back to the island or spend the night standing on the coral heads.

They decided to try to swim, they slipped back into the lagoon, buttocks tightened by the certainty that brother shark was looking up at them. When they finally clambered ashore they were feeling heroic. They told us about the watery adventure, then showered and we gathered for dinner.

There was cake for dessert to celebrate the boys' successful return. With a flourish Marlon served each of the children a large piece. As they were about to devour it, Marlon swept the cake off everybody's plate onto his and in a matter of seconds ate it all. He made it fun for them. He cut them another piece. When Marlon is at peace with himself—and that is most likely when he's in the South Pacific—he is a congenial, inventive, and sensitive companion, the finest friend and father to be found anywhere.

I watched Christian through the years as he tried different trades—gardening, tree surgery, painting, welding. He had no great success, but he developed one skill at which he is better than anyone else alive. Reading Marlon Brando. The circumstances of his life so often depended on Marlon's mood that Christian spent time honing this faculty.

Marlon and I were talking one night in his bedroom and Christian came in. He wanted to go out for the evening and he wanted money. But he didn't mention either. The psychological food to feed Marlon was to tell him, "Dad, I know how you want me to behave and I'm doing it, don't worry. I know the system in the house and I know my part in it." Underscore that Marlon is a diligent father, serious but understanding. Christian got all this across without saying a word, just his body positions.

Simultaneously, his intelligence gathering began. Under his cap-tipping shyness, Christian was ripping through Marlon's pockets, his drawers, the papers on his desk, the reading matter by his bed, his brain. Christian's eyes darted and flickered like the blinking light on a computer. In nanoseconds he had scanned Marlon's mood, voice level, timbre, body position, physiognomy. His readout was a complete profile on Marlon at that instant. All this had occurred during the time it took Christian in a kind young man's voice to say, "Dave and I were thinking of going to a movie. Is that okay, Dad?"

I marveled at Christian's adroitness. After he left I imitated him and Marlon saw what I had seen, we replayed the scene to each other. If there were awards given for working your parents, staying under their radar, making them feel good about you for that local minute when you wanted a yes from them, Christian would have an Oscar on his shelf. He might have saved MGM millions of dollars if he'd been on the *Mutiny* set. Christian couldn't always tell you why Marlon was going to do something, but he'd tell you exactly when he was about to do it.

On television I saw that Christian had shot and killed Dag Drollet in Marlon's house. I left a message on Marlon's answering machine that I had heard, to call me when it was right.

A couple of days later he called. He'd been consumed by his dealings with the police, the press, the attorneys, handling the pile of details. For the next two years our long telephone talks were more frequent and filled with discussions about Christian and Cheyenne.

I don't know what Marlon decided in the first moments after the shooting about how he would act and what his attitude toward Christian would be. I didn't know then and I don't know now. I saw the stress in him as Christian's story unfolded over the next months. I felt for Marlon and was his companion during those difficult months, but no one knew better than I that you go through those events alone.

I want to be careful to express my sadness and sorrow for both Marlon and Christian, I want not to criticize for I have no idea what the best course of action would have been. But I did have thoughts different from Marlon's, some of them I told him, they are subjective and are statements of feelings, not knowledge.

Marlon said that on the night of the killing Christian came to the house to take his half sister Cheyenne to dinner. Before he arrived he'd drunk a six-pack of malt liquor and started on hard liquor. He also brought a gun of Marlon's that Marlon wanted returned to the house. Christian and Cheyenne went to Musso and Frank's on Hollywood Boulevard. There, Cheyenne, who was more than six months pregnant with Dag's child, told Christian that Dag was physically abusing her, apparently she stressed the point. After dinner they went back to Marlon's.

In the large guest living room, Dag was watching television. Cheyenne introduced Christian to her six-three 270-pound boyfriend; they hadn't met before. Cheyenne went to her room and Christian went into Marlon's room at the other end of the house and sat with Marlon, who was watching television. They said very little, Marlon told me, just watched the tube.

About forty-five minutes later Christian rose and left the room. In a few moments he was back, standing in the doorway.

"I killed Dag, he's dead, Pop. I didn't mean to do it. He went for the gun and it went off."

Marlon ran out of his room, down the hall to the living room, through the dining room, the kitchen, to the other living room. Marlon tried to revive Dag, gave him mouth-to-mouth resuscitation. No dice. Marlon called 911.

Christian was charged with first-degree murder. He came to court handcuffed, unshaven, and wearing a gray shirt and jeans. The lawyer William Kunstler, an old friend of Marlon's, appeared with him.

"The shooting was an accident, the result of a scuffle between Christian and Dag Drollet," Kunstler said. "Christian is innocent of the murder charge, this is not murder by any means."

The Los Angeles police said there was no indication there had been a struggle. Dag Drollet's position was not combative, he was sitting back holding a cigarette lighter in one hand, the channel selector in the other. The shot had been fired at close range. It was first-degree murder, they said.

In tapes recorded after the shooting, Christian told the police, "I said, 'Hold on, wait . . . and kablammo! Something hit—I don't know if I hit the trigger or if he hit the trigger, who knows? I didn't want to shoot the guy, no way. I got too much to lose. I got my job, my business, my house. I'd been drinking, you know, I was drunk, I will admit to that. I was blasted." Christian also said, "I hated that motherfucker."

Cheyenne told the police that the shooting was not an accident, it was premeditated.

Jacques Drollet found out he'd lost his son when someone
from *Hard Copy* called him in Tahiti. Reporters camped outside Marlon's compound, helicopters circled above, and car-
loads of people stopped to gawk.

Marlon talked calmly as he told me what he'd been
through. We talked of Bryan and of Paul Newman's son,
Scott, who also died of drugs.

I told Marlon that when Bryan died, along with the tor-
ment, I stood still to consider what had led to the tragedy so I
would never let such a thing happen again. I recommended
that before deciding on a course of action, Marlon stop and
study all the paths running into the moment when Christian
shot Dag, then decide what to do. If Christian's life had been
dominated by Marlon and Marlon's celebrity, and if that had
something to do with his shooting Dag, this would be the
time to know it. It might be best for Christian to have Marlon's love and support but to have charge of his own life.

Marlon made his own decisions about Christian's defense.
He picked and paid for the lawyers, he established the strategy and managed the case. Christian seemed in a way not
really to be the principal, he was a sort of a tree stump people
walked around and pointed at.

After three months in jail, Christian was released on two
million dollars bail for which Marlon put up his house.
Christian had begun working as a welder and appearing for
random drug checks.

Christian's hearing, in which he would plead guilty to the charge of voluntary manslaughter, was set for February 26, 1991.

"I've been coming through these doors since I was a kid," he said as he entered the Santa Monica Courthouse. He was referring to the many times he'd come when Marlon and Anna were having their vitriolic brawls over his custody.

Asked whether his relationship with his father had changed because of the shooting of Dag Drollet, Christian answered, "No, he's been helping me through this, supporting me as a friend . . . and who am I, I'm a nobody."

Apparently the defense strategy was to picture Christian as drug-controlled and not competent. A sorrowful picture was drawn.

His psychiatrist, Dr. Saul Faerstein, said, "Once an inquisitive and alert child, Christian has been damaged by his upbringing and chronic substance abuse. Despite the material advantages conferred by the Brando name, neither parent provided a stable, protective, safe, emotional environment for Christian to grow up in."

His probation officer said: "Mr. Brando has suffered brain damage from drug and alcohol abuse as a youth. His early years were marked by custody battles between his mother and his father. He was kidnapped several times by one or the other of his parents, molested by a hired kidnapper, and abused by his alcoholic, mentally ill mother. Christian is unassuming, low-profile, low-self-esteemed."

An alcoholism expert estimated that Christian's alcohol level at the time of the shooting was at least 0.27—more than three times the legal limit in California.

Christian said about himself, "I grew up with an extremely

violent mother. She drank, we had a lot of problems. My whole family except for my father is alcoholic—my family's so weird and spaced out. We'd have new additions all the time. Like I'd sit down at the table with all these strange people and say, 'Who are you?' "

Christian reconsidered what Cheyenne had told him. "She went off on this bizarre tangent, she kinda like got me going, I didn't stop to think. Knowing what I know now of her mental state, I doubt whether she was ever beaten by Drollet. I feel like a complete chump for believing her."

The testimony about Christian's mother was appalling. Anna Kashfi left Marlon a year after they were married, taking Christian, five months old, with her.

Virginia Hardy, who had befriended Christian when he was eleven, said at times he begged her to stay with him until he was safe in bed.

"One night," Hardy said, "Kashfi got up in the middle of the night, went into her son's bedroom, snatched him from a deep sleep, and slapped him continuously, saying, 'I want you to apologize to me! I want you to apologize to me!'

"Christian said, 'What did I do wrong?' Not getting an answer, he said, 'Okay, I apologize, I apologize!'

"His mother then demanded, 'Why are you patronizing me?' "

I attended one long session with Marlon, Christian, and Robert Shapiro, the attorney who had replaced William Kunstler. Marlon had great animosity toward the attorneys conducting the prosecution. That was understandable to me, but at the same time Marlon's anger seemed unreasonable. Of course the prosecutors would go after Christian, he'd killed a man.

During the meeting Christian said almost nothing. He was in the most fateful situation of his life yet he was having no effect on its outcome. Marlon controlled everything. Unable or not allowed to contribute, Christian listened to the talk, mainly Marlon's, his feelings not plumbed, his voice not heard.

A couple of times he said, "Dad, what's going to happen, am I going to jail?" as if Marlon had control over that, too. It didn't seem right to me. Christian was thirty-two, why wasn't he treated as a grown-up, why was he so completely outside the discussions and decisions? Wasn't this repeating and compounding the circumstances that had brought his life to this point?

Marlon testified on the third and last day of Christian's hearing. Newspaper headlines said it would be the performance of his life. I think Marlon meant for it to be, feeling he could pick up all the marbles if he delivered a stem-winding performance that day. My guess is that he took a couple of Valium.

"No, I will not swear to God because I don't believe in the conventional God," Marlon began. "I will swear on the lives of my children and my grandchildren."

He began by talking of his marriage to Anna Kashfi. "She was probably the most beautiful woman I have ever met. I think there must be some rewarding aspects to all people, but Christian's mother is close to being as negative and as cruel a person as I have met in this world."

Marlon described Christian as "a basket case of emotional disorders. You always tend to blame the other parent, but I know I could have done better. I think perhaps I failed as a father, but I did the best I could."

Shapiro asked Marlon for background on Christian's drinking habits. Marlon said, "I come from a long line of Irish drunks. My great-uncle Miles O'Gunn was a drunk. Both of my sisters were drunks. I have been to Alcoholics Anonymous meetings with my mother and my father. But I have never abused any kind of substance—maybe food, I guess." Laughter from the audience. "That'll appear in the papers," he added.

He brought another laugh from the packed courtroom when he was asked if Christian had ever lied to him.

"That guy knows how to lie better than I do, but he can't lie to me worth a damn. With the girls it's different, I'm sorry to say. But there again, we all lie to the girls, don't we, Judge?"

Abruptly, Marlon turned to the Drollet family and spoke to them in French. "You are the grandfather and grandmother of the baby, and I am also the grandfather of the baby. Even if I am in the cinema, don't mistake my emotions for acting . . . we can't continue with enmity in our eyes and our hearts."

He choked back tears when he talked about the killing. "As much as it may not be believed, I loved Dag. He was going to be the father of my grandchild. As they were carrying the body out, I asked one of the officers to unzip the bag because I wanted to say good-bye to him properly. I kissed him and told him I loved him."

Marlon spoke for seventy-five minutes. Dag Drollet's mother and father were there each day of the hearing and they were there for this one. Jacques Drollet, who had known Marlon for thirty years, was asked what he thought of Marlon's testimony.

"Brando is an actor, he can cry and lie like a horse can run, he was acting, does anyone believe a word of it?"

I was not at the court but I read the transcript. I found myself in agreement with Jacques Drollet: Marlon was acting. Maybe, like the monk in "The Story of the Juggler of Our Lady," he was giving to Christian the one thing he knew how to do best, his acting talent. But this wasn't the greatest actor of his time seizing everyone's imagination, this was a former champion, overweight, out of shape, sloppy with his technique.

Marlon might have burned up that little theater in the good days; he could well have given the performance of his life, shown the audience the fantastic theatrical experience he could provide. But to me it didn't seem like a time for theater, it didn't seem the occasion for Christian's father to take the microphone and do a medley of his emotions.

Christian was sentenced to ten years in prison.

Depicting Christian as damaged from drugs and abuse when he was a child was an effective defense. Yet I wasn't convinced that Christian was impaired to the degree the experts described. I wondered how this collection of descriptions would affect him.

The judge and attorneys were convened to decide Christian Brando's fate, but the Santa Monica courtroom was Marlon's stage. The public saw a deeply concerned father, a man damaged by events but unwavering in his loyalty to his children.

Whatever else Marlon had in mind, in portraying himself as so loyal to his son and so bereft at the death of Dag Drollet, he silenced the question most likely to be raised.

"Mr. Brando, your daughter Cheyenne has made repeated suicide attempts and is in psychiatric care, your son Christian murdered her boyfriend in your house. Without wanting to put too great a burden on you at this time, what does that say about you as a parent?"

The question has hardly been mentioned. Even with an acting job that only faintly recalls what he's capable of, Marlon kept it to a murmur.

A significant amount of the communication between Marlon and me was by telephone, all through the years our lives were thick with phone calls. Marlon especially, and particularly in his later years, spent major chunks of his waking hours on the phone. Sometimes our conversations were discursive and rambling, sometimes they were about fundamental things.

A week before Christian shot Dag Drollet, I arrived late in the day at my Santa Monica apartment, there were three messages from Marlon. The first just said to call him. The second was longer.

He said: "I'll call you back shortly, that's the biggest lie you've ever told. It's me checking in and checking out. I called my sister up and made peace with her over an argument we had. It was good to resolve things with Titty because it's not what we do, it's how we're able to forgive ourselves and others that marks our advancement in this mottled journey. Thinking about you, we don't chum up as often as we used to, but I guess we're built into the wallpaper now. Bless you, my fair-haired lad, wish you well, and I'll talk to you in Palm Springs. You're probably in Istanbul or someplace."

No real substance, just Marlon's mind going crabwise across the roof, but I sensed worry. When something troubles Marlon he often doesn't just say it. He talks about your life first, then he'll put his chip on the table.

The third message was: "I don't want one ounce, I don't want one milligram of bullshit from you. I know you're there sitting across the room thinking, Shall I get on the phone and talk to Marlon—nah, maybe later. I can hear the TV in the background, so answer the phone. Don't give me any shit that you're on the john or you had to run downstairs to argue with the postman. Pick it up and talk because I don't need a Butterfinger, I don't need a Milky Way, I don't need any Jujubes, what I need is a Snicker. I know, you're out to lunch with the ambassador from Saudi Arabia making an oil deal, but I do want to talk to you, a few practical details but mostly wanting to hear your dulcet tones. So feel good and stick it up your ass and I'll try you later."

I settled on the bed and called him back. Marlon often recorded his phone conversations and urged me to do it, too. Once in a while I did. I recorded this one.

MARLON: Where you been?

GEORGE: Trying to start a career in television.

MARLON: Did you get dressed up so you'd look handsome?

GEORGE: Oh yeah, nice sweater, shirt made in Rome, if you're going to pursue the meaningless it's important to dress well.

MARLON: Who'd you see?

GEORGE: Very important executive, my future as a producer may hang on that meeting, wish I remembered his name.

MARLON: No career for you. I achieved success because I always remember names and faces . . . who am I talking to again?

GEORGE: You're talking to the guy who said this. 'Think back to a hundred years ago and what do you see? Men and women busy marrying, bringing up children, sickening, dying, fighting, feasting, farming, flattering, grumbling at fate. Of all that life, not a trace survives. Even to men whose lives were a blaze of glory, this comes to pass. We must aspire, then, to this and this alone: the just thought, the unselfish act, the tongue that utters no falsehood.' Who said it?

MARLON: Rock Hudson.

GEORGE: Jesus, that's scary, you are so close.

MARLON: Wait, don't tell me, I know, Merv Griffin.

GEORGE: I have to give you a partially correct because for sure you'd have said it in the next breath. Marcus Aurelius, the *Meditations*.

MARLON: Shit, then Merv Griffin should have counted, Marcus and Merv are practically the same person.

GEORGE: That's why I'm giving you a partial, you only missed it by twenty centuries.

MARLON: I read those *Meditations* when I lived in New York. Same time I was reading Thorstein Veblen's *Theory of the Leisure Class*.

GEORGE: Think of it, Mar, almost two thousand years ago this Roman emperor decided to jot down his thoughts on life while he was in the palace, bivouacked in battle, everywhere. And I'm getting help from reading them today.

MARLON: What else are you reading?

GEORGE: Same as you, *The Enquirer*. It's Wednesday, has your copy arrived yet?

MARLON: No, and I need it for the puppies to pee on.

GEORGE: There's always some good stuff about you. "Troubled Brando Takes Six Enemas a Day."

MARLON: See, they don't know, it's eight.

GEORGE: Here's a good line. It's from a book called *Chance and Necessity* by Jacques Monod, French biologist, won the Nobel Prize for science. "Man knows at last that he is alone in the Universe's unfeeling immensity. His destiny is nowhere spelled out, nor is his duty."

MARLON: Oh, that's perfect for you. Alone in the Universe's unfeeling immensity, that's the picture you've got because you've always been without a father.

GEORGE: I suppose, all the serious stuff in my life gets back to that. But I think he's scientifically right also. We've been out in space now, been to the moon, we orbit the earth for three months at a time, nobody's ever bumped into heaven.

MARLON: It's not there, it never was there. But you're not attracted to those words because of their scientific accuracy; they match your feelings. What was the last part, our duty isn't spelled out?

GEORGE: Yeah.

MARLON: That's what attracts you, you're not certain what your duty is. Remember how shocked I was when you told me you once considered staying in the navy.

GEORGE: Yes.

MARLON: You said because navy life had a form, the paths were marked, you knew what your duty was. I can hear what that biologist said, I can think he said it well, but it has no emotion for me. There's no God, there's no heaven, ho-hum. You're always looking into the meaning of life, but tonight it's going to have to wait, we're going to talk about my problem—Cheyenne.

GEORGE: What about her?

MARLON: She's doing Ophelia, crooning madrigals as she glides down the river in a boat with no oars.

GEORGE: Is it real?

MARLON: That's the question.

GEORGE: Is that why you brought her over from Tahiti?

MARLON: Yeah, she started having violent outbursts, mood shifts, unpredictable behavior.

GEORGE: That's hard to believe, your daughter showing unpredictable behavior?

MARLON: I brought her here for evaluation, she didn't want to come but her boyfriend, Dag Drollet, persuaded her.

GEORGE: Nice guy?

MARLON: Tahitian. Yeah, good guy, I've known his family for thirty years. Tarita's here, too. [Tarita is Marlon's former wife, Cheyenne's mother.]

GEORGE: All staying at the house?

MARLON: Of course.

GEORGE: So how's Cheyenne acting?

MARLON: She suddenly goes vague, just isn't there, then she'll start screaming.

GEORGE: At you?

MARLON: At whoever. Or whatever. Why don't you come up, I'd like to know what you see.

GEORGE: How is she reacting to the evaluations?

MARLON: She does the same thing there, acts odd. You can see she's doing loco, but exactly what kind you can't say for sure.

GEORGE: I'll come up.

MARLON: It'll be helpful. Don't act like I suggested it.

GEORGE: No, I know what to do.

Two evenings later I went up to Marlon's house. After the three of us spent a while together, he left Cheyenne and me alone. We talked calmly and easily. I realized that though I'd seen her intermittently, I had never spent any real time with her. She was a delicate riddle. First, she was luminously pretty, not large but with an almost aggressive beauty, black hair, dark eyes, and in those eyes an anima pulsing.

I became fascinated—in Marlon's female child I was seeing the same penetrating stare, the offhand sexuality, the eyes that know—all the Brando hallmarks. That dark disdainful look Marlon has turned on so many adversaries comes through her eyes, often, I noticed, when they are turned on him. Cheyenne has Marlon's ability to manipulate and control.

Marlon's will to have things his way is almost unopposable. His acting ability, his storytelling, his doggedness finally bend you. But in the unlikely event those techniques don't work, he goes to the major weapon, abandonment of the whole civilized code. His face can show such anger, such threat of anarchy if you don't accede to what he's demanding that you do. No one has ever matched him in this threat to bring the empire down. No one till now.

When she doesn't take her medicine, and even sometimes when she does, Cheyenne is given to screaming fits. The screams are chilling heralds of the mad zone she seems close to entering. The wilderness and horror of this implied world keep you from doing anything that will push her toward it. You do not want to witness her crossing that threshold. You wait for a cue about what you should do—or not do—to assure she doesn't. You are controlled by her behavior.

Is her behavior real or is it feigned? Could it be feigned, could anyone act all that? Hard to imagine, who would have the guts to behave in such a way? Perhaps only someone who had hung around Marlon Brando for years or happened to be his child. Then it would be possible.

The world's greatest living actor was troubled by an acting problem—he was unable to determine whether his daughter was in the grasp of fearful interior forces, or whether he was the captive audience at her one-woman show.

"She's your kid, Mar," I said after Cheyenne had gone to bed. "The similarities between you are both sobering and funny. But she's younger, Mar, and stronger, she's going to lead you up the hills and down the valleys, you're going to be puffing, man."

He laughed. "If she was your kid, what would you do?"

"Wait."

"For what?"

"Until it was clear what was wrong. I wouldn't administer a cure until I knew for sure what the illness was. It could be she misses her father."

"Well, we know something is wrong, she's definitely acting odd, that's why she's here."

"What I see, Mar, is someone who's lived a freaky life and has learned techniques that work in that life. It would be nice to see her in a normal neighborhood for a while with a normal job, normal boyfriend, nobody taking her shopping, nobody catering to her, no drugs."

"I'd like to see that, too."

We didn't come to a conclusion, we decided I'd come back in a few days and talk with Cheyenne again. We didn't have that second meeting because three nights later Christian came to take Cheyenne to dinner at Musso and Frank's.

Cheyenne went back to Tahiti very soon after the killing. Because she was sued in Tahiti by the Drollet family as an accessory to the death of Dag, she was not allowed to leave the island. Suicide attempts and erratic outbursts continued.

Once Christian was sent to prison in Chino, Marlon turned his attention back to Cheyenne. He wanted to get her out of Tahiti so she could be treated in the United States. The judge in Tahiti, a man named Gotti, would not allow her to leave. Marlon could not go back to Tahiti because he was also named in the Drollets' suit and could easily be detained there.

Finally, Cheyenne was released to go to France for treatment. Marlon first rented a villa in the country then later an apartment in Paris to be with her.

"I'll stay with Cheyenne until she's well, I have to," he told me.

We had nearly as many long conversations while he was in France as we did when he was in Beverly Hills. They had mostly to do with Cheyenne, but sometimes it was just talk. This day Marlon sounded low, I wanted to lighten his mood.

"Getting any zook?" I asked.

"Nothing so far, maybe the maid," Marlon said.

"The French maid. Every schoolboy's fantasy."

"Nothing's happened yet, I'm watching. I look up from my *Figaro* when she passes."

"How do you go about seducing the maid, hold out a nosegay and smile shyly when she's doing the toilet bowls? Before I get carried away, Mar, what does she look like?"

"Porky."

"Porky?"

"From the local village. Creditable ass. It's a possible, she may not be up for it."

How cruel is age. This sexual colossus who with a phone call could once have lured the lady in any household to his lair was questioning whether the clunky charwoman from the village would consent to congress with him.

"How's Cheyenne?"

"Good when she takes the medicine. If she doesn't take it, she gets violent, throws things at me."

"So it's physical now."

"Oh yeah, if she doesn't take the pills she's a samurai. Then she suddenly isolates herself."

Cheyenne was installed in a clinic and allowed to spend weekends with Marlon. After two months she was moved to another clinic, but it still was not clear what was wrong.

Cheyenne was away from the clinic for longer and longer periods, she stayed at Marlon's house against the rules set by the court. The police came one morning at 5 A.M. and found something like a party going on. They removed Cheyenne and sent her back to Tahiti.

Marlon returned to L.A. and renewed his efforts to get Cheyenne to the United States. Several months later she appeared in court in Papeete. Her behavior was so bizarre that she was released to come to the United States. The end of a long journey for Marlon. Or so it seemed. In fact, it was only the appearance of good news, for Cheyenne brought the full theater of her eccentricities with her. Marlon had planned to get her a place in Hawaii where she could be tranquil. It didn't work, she was soon back in his house. He was faced again with the problem of where and with whom she would live.

It had been two devastating years for Marlon. He called me on a Sunday morning, low and in despair.

"I've just got to face it, got to get used to it. If she's going to kill herself, I can't stop it. Christ, it's awful to have that hanging over you every waking hour. And every sleeping hour."

"Mar, you've been doing coolie work with both Christian and Cheyenne, the sad thing, the noticeable thing, is your efforts haven't changed anything. They've got to take charge of their lives, the longer they go without doing it the harder it's going to be for them."

"You don't know where the trail stops. I thought once I got Cheyenne out of Tahiti the mission was over."

"I'm concerned about you now. Mar, I want you to explore the sunny side of life. Feeling good and having fun seem like distant memories, get them cranked up again."

After a half hour of talk the results were good.

"I feel better, I was in bad shape, Georgie, I'm definitely starting to feel better."

Weeks later Marlon commented again on that phone call, saying the idea of enjoying life had gotten through.

What are the results of Marlon's efforts? Cheyenne has given interviews sharply critical of Marlon, accused him of having sexual interest in her. She says that had she been at Christian's trial, she would have said "that my father was responsible for the death of my fiancé . . . my father told Christian to bring the gun to the house that night." She comments further about Marlon. "He is a very powerful man. He's the Godfather in the flesh, capable of manipulating others as he wants . . ."

More sad days were ahead for Marlon: Christian went to prison for seven years, Cheyenne committed suicide.

10

Six months after Christian killed Dag Drollet in 1990, Marlon called and asked me to come to the house, there was something he wanted to discuss. We sat in his bedroom, in the sitting area by the fireplace. The television was on, Marlon turned it off.

"I'm going to write my autobiography," he said. "I want you to be the agent for it."

I had read about it, his attorney, Belinda Frixou, in England, had given some press releases about it. Why? was my first thought. Marlon disdained autobiographies, he called them self-serving junk, he ridiculed the movie stars that wrote them.

"I've been thinking a lot about it," he went on. "You've never been an agent, but you know me best. I think you can represent me better than anyone."

"Mar, I think you should get Mort Janklow; he's a friend

of mine and probably the best. He's already sent me a note saying he'd like to represent your book."

"No," Marlon said quickly. "Swifty Lazar wants to represent it, too. I don't want any of those guys, no agents or lawyers, I don't trust any of them. I'd like you to do it."

"Okay."

I believed he was right. If he was truly going to write his autobiography, no one could sell it better than I.

"Why are you writing it?" I asked.

"For the kids. I realized during these court appearances how much of a mystery I am to Christian—who is my father, who is Marlon Brando? Being a celebrity in this culture distorts everything. They write anything they want and keep repeating it; your kids don't know what's true. Later on, when they want to know something about me, they can read my book; they won't have to go to old copies of film magazines."

It had a reasonable sound, but somehow it didn't seem a real reason, at least not a complete one. And even if it was the real reason, I wasn't sure it would be strong enough to carry him through the long process of actually writing the story of his life. But the idea of Marlon writing his autobiography was an attractive one, I was for that.

"How much do you think they'll pay?" he asked.

There was the reason, or at least a big part of it. Money was an important factor, maybe the most important factor, to Marlon those days.

"Depends on whether you'll actually write it."

"I *am* going to write it."

"They have to believe you're going to write it."

"You convince them, tell them exactly what I'm going to write."

"What are you going to write?"

"Everything."

"What's everything?"

"Yeah, what's everything? I won't exclude anything, though."

"The women in your life?"

"I'm not going to write the lurid crap where some movie star gives a list of the actresses he's fucked. And I won't talk about Sono . . . But I won't leave out any important things. I may change names."

"Your children? Christian's trial?"

"The kids, I don't know. I'll talk to them."

"There's already been talk about your autobiography, your lawyer in England announced it. The way it was handled, it seemed you were floating a balloon to see how much money was out there. I didn't think that was good. If you're going to write your autobiography, the project should be handled with dignity."

"I agree. You do it."

"If I do it, I have to be the only one doing it, no lawyers or anybody else talking about it."

"It'll be just you, that's what I want."

I suggested that he send a letter to the publishers I'd select saying he was writing his book and I was his representative. If they had interest in the project, they should contact me. I wrote the letter and he signed it.

At our next meeting I said, "I want to be clear with the publishers about what we're selling, I think we should write down exactly what the book will contain and what it won't. It's not for anyone else to see, just so you and I understand precisely what I'm going to be selling." He agreed.

Some of the discussion that followed was numbingly long; Marlon would agree to certain elements being included then back up and circle around. He'd chew on the cud for a while then finally commit when I pointed out that the event we were talking about was too central to his life to be left out of his autobiography. Finally we produced the necessary document.

We discussed what I should be paid. Marlon led off and talked for several minutes; what he said was a jumble. I said it seemed to be pretty straightforward business, agents are usually paid a fee of ten percent. Marlon gave a brisk response, but literally neither he nor I could follow what he was saying. Finally he called Alice in to take down our discussion. She dutifully recorded every word we said, twelve pages of it. It could be two inmates in a bide-a-wee talking. This is part of it.

MARLON: The following conversation is between George Englund and myself, and it's about points of interest along the way toward the creation of this book which should be remembered and recorded forever. Okay, here we go, George and I around the track. Good morning. The money. I think that the money should be relevant to, I think it should not be less than, ah, well, first of all I want to think about what time is going to be involved in getting this deal settled, I think that not less than two hundred thousand would be a good figure and that should upscale in direct proportion to the amount of money the book makes, it will rise . . .

GEORGE: You're talking about my deal now?

MARLON: Yes.

GEORGE: You're saying a floor of two hundred thousand?

MARLON: Right.

GEORGE: Against what? At what rate?

MARLON: At one percent. One percent of five hundred thousand is what? Fifty thousand dollars—or—I don't know whether two percent would be a hundred thousand. Well, let's call it two percent because I'm sure that the book is certainly going to make a hundred thousand dollars and that will include the rights to television, film . . .

GEORGE: Two percent?

MARLON: If we talk about that it makes sense.

GEORGE: A guarantee of two hundred thousand against two percent, is that what you're saying?

MARLON: Yeah. Two percent, two hundred thousand of five million is what? Two percent.

GEORGE: Four percent.

MARLON: Four percent?

GEORGE: Four percent of five million is two hundred thousand.

MARLON: Yes, that would be four percent. So I think that's sufficient considering the fact that you've not, it's not going to be a sliding scale, you're going to get right off the top in the cream area, you're going to get two hundred thousand dollars plus whatever it's going to make at one percent.

GEORGE: One percent of what, gross, net?

MARLON: I would guess whatever they pay.

GEORGE: They? There are different kinds of deals. But one percent of the net of something would be confiscatory.

MARLON: What does *confiscatory* mean?

GEORGE: *Confiscatory* means that the possibilities of making any profit with one percent of the net are nonexistent. You don't take net deals, Mar, you have gross deals.

MARLON: I have gross deals.

GEORGE: Yes.

MARLON: I'll give you a gross deal.

GEORGE: Okay.

MARLON: All right, let's say it again. It's two hundred thousand win, lose, or draw. If I drop dead, well, if you don't perform, there's no reason for me to pay you.

GEORGE: Ha, ha, ha, what does that mean?

MARLON: That means if you drop dead, I don't have to pay your estate.

GEORGE: What does *perform* mean?

MARLON: *Perform* means to do the job of doing this . . . now I've taken a chance on love here because I want to give you the money, although you haven't asked me for money, I just had a feeling that you were, you know, bouncing along wondering whether or not you should do this script or do the other script and I had a feeling that all is not well in your camp, don't know if that's true.

GEORGE: Let's not connect these two things. This book is a

big piece of business and it deserves full-time concentration. If I am appropriate to do that, then okay.

MARLON: I don't know if you're appropriate to do that.

GEORGE: Well, then what are we doing?

MARLON: No, I want you to do it because I believe that you can do it, because I believe I can do it: And you're better at doing things like that than I am, I would guess, I don't know . . . wait a minute, there's another thing we've left out of this, which is you as a contributor to this story. If the book goes, you'll get a hundred thousand dollars for writing your chapter; if the book does not go, you'll get a guarantee of fifty thousand dollars.

GEORGE: If what I write is not in the book.

MARLON: Yeah, I guess that would have to be the guarantee. So you're going to get two hundred fifty thousand dollars guaranteed. Unless there is an act of God.

Basically, Marlon didn't want to pay the normal agent's commission of ten percent. Later in the conversation he said I should receive five percent. That engendered the following exchange.

"Mar, the reason you asked me to be your agent is because you believe I can do the job better than anyone else. True?"

"Yes."

"Then why isn't it proper to pay me the normal rate?"

"No, five percent is right."

"Why?"

"You've never done it before."

"All right, let's look at that. There are hundreds of agents who make book deals every day, you don't want any of them."

"No."

"So how many times the agent's done it before isn't the criterion."

"That's right."

"Who you believe will do it best is the criterion."

"That's right."

"And that's me."

"Right."

"Think what you're saying: 'I can have any agent in the world, but I believe so strongly that George can do it better than anybody else, I'm going to pay him half the normal fee."

"Agents don't do anything, I make all my own deals, I could do this myself and save all the money, but you can do it better. Five percent."

The wrangling could go on forever and if it did the whole thing would likely dissolve. I didn't want that, this was appealing, a new field, a new project, it was more important to me than the five percent.

"We've triumphed, Mar, we've avoided the one great peril that I might be overpaid."

"Do it, Georgie, put on your pointed Cuban shoes, get out your malacca cane, and go over there and sell the book."

There was something else I wanted to say. "We've always been competitive, Mar. This king-of-the-hill stuff still goes on, but in this project it doesn't exist. This book is your life, you lived it, you own it. My role is to get the book sold, I'll do that the best way I know how."

"Great, Georgie. That's all there is to say."

There was still the question in my mind about what was

really in his mind, why he wanted to write his autobiography. I believed money to be one reason; beyond that, I wasn't sure that even Marlon was sure.

All the publishers who received Marlon's letter responded. From all there was curiosity. From some who had tried to pursue the project when the book was first bruited about by Ms. Frixou, there was frustration; they felt they'd been forced into a nonsense game and didn't know whether to believe I was representing his book or not.

They were right; Ms. Frixou is a lovely person and, as Marlon believed, a superior attorney, but she knew little about book publishing.

The first thing I did when I went to New York was talk to Mort Janklow. We had breakfast at the Regency. I told him that although I'd recommended him to Marlon, Marlon had decided on someone else. Me. I remember well his response.

"George, you know how much I would love to have represented Marlon, and I thank you for trying. But I can understand he wants somebody close to him, someone he trusts. Good luck, I'm here, don't hesitate to call, I'll be any help I can."

I asked his idea of what would be the largest advance I could get. He thought awhile. "It's a tough one, George, most books I could probably guess within ten percent. The publishers are going to—let me take that back, the publishers *should* ask hard questions. They're going to have to buy it without seeing a word written . . . I'd guess probably two and a half, maybe three million—maybe. You'll have to get out there and see. You'll earn your money."

Mort was right, there was a lot of skepticism.

"Who knows if he can write? Yeah, he's a great actor, but that's not writing, especially it's not writing a whole book," said one.

"Some people can write a newspaper column, some a magazine article, and do it well. Most of the time they can't do a book, it's a whole different piece of work."

"To me, celebrity autobiographies are almost always worthless," said the president of one company. "We made a deal with Rex Harrison, he worked on his autobiography for a year and a half then handed us thirty-six pages. 'This isn't a book,' I said, 'where's the rest?' 'There'll be a lot of pictures,' Harrison's agent said."

"I wouldn't offer you much until I saw something," said another. "Anyway, I doubt he'll ever write it. It'll turn out like one of his movie deals; maybe the picture gets made, but it turns out lousy and it cost too much."

Smart observations, I had to be artful to persuade around them.

After each meeting with a publisher, Marlon wanted to hear the details. He'd come alive, we'd spend an entire dinner doing improvisations about people I was telling him about that he hadn't even met.

He said he wanted me to wear a microphone and tape the meetings. Then he wanted me to videotape them.

"Tell them it's for legal purposes, to make sure everything is understood," he said.

I laughed. "That's impossible, Mar."

"You can do it."

"Mar, they'd think I was crazy if I showed up with a video camera."

"Tell them I'm quirky, I want to see who I'd be working with."

"You quirky, who's going to believe that?"

"Okay, then don't even talk about it, just do it."

"Let's see, I come into the publisher's office wearing my good suit and carrying a Samsonite case. I say, 'Before we start, be a love and hand me that tripod, would you? There's a dear.'"

"Then put a light meter in his face," Marlon adds.

"Right, and mind if I put a dab of rouge on this mole? Then the publisher calls security and I'm airlifted to a psychiatric hospital."

Marlon was particularly fascinated with my description of the woman editor who insisted she knew all about him. I'd said that Marlon is complex, she shouldn't consider she had real knowledge of him from reading his publicity.

"Don't worry, I know all about Brando, I know exactly what kind of editor he needs," she said authoritatively.

"Yes, and how do you know him so completely?"

"I read the Capote article in *The New Yorker,* now that was real, see, Brando was talking in his own voice, he didn't do his funny stuff, no crap about the Indians, he didn't even try to disguise anything. Tell you the truth, I don't think he knew Capote was taking notes. That's where I learned about Brando."

"I see, but that was written thirty years ago and the piece was only a few pages long."

"Sure, people don't change, you think people change? I know who Brando is."

"That's pretty good going. Because Brando's not certain

who Brando is. You be sure and fill him in when he gets to town."

"You really say that?" Marlon asked with delight.

"Yeah, she was so arrogant. You could never have worked with her. They don't have the money anyway."

I met Harold Evans, president of Random House. From the beginning he was keen to have Marlon's book. Physically and conversationally Harry bustles; he darts in and out of the office while you're talking, and while en route he changes conversational directions like a quarter horse. But with all the agitato, Harry held a calm eye on the problems attached to Marlon's book.

"These are the questions facing me," he said. "Will Brando actually write it, can Brando actually write, will Brando actually tell about himself, his children, his women?"

"Your questions are definitely the right ones," I said, "and to be perfectly honest, I have to say there's no guarantee of a yes answer to any of them."

"That's bad, you don't want to start a project like this with doubts."

"But the success of the book won't depend wholly on Marlon," I said. "The abilities of the publishing house will count for a lot. Marlon's got to be in the right home, he's got to be in the company of people who understand him and can work with him to get the book done."

"Yes, good, let's say Random House will be that home."

"Knowing Marlon as I do, I can tell you his publisher will have to be in superb form to get the book that is really inside him."

"We have everything to do that, the best editors, I have

somebody wonderful in mind . . . I'm not sure exactly what you mean."

"I don't know if you follow American football, Harry, but when you give a quarterback a fifty-million-dollar contract, you don't send him out and tell him just throw the football. You put the biggest, fastest offensive line you can buy in front of him. Something like that is what's needed for Marlon."

"I'm certain that part is right; he'll need very good help. I'd give him that personally," Harry said.

"You know more about this than I, Harry, but I notice that often people don't know what the great moments in their lives are, someone has to draw them out. And sometimes people are reluctant to talk about very personal things. Marlon will be."

"Quite correct. I want to assure you we would be better than anyone at that."

I felt Harry should meet Marlon, they could be a good pairing. Before setting up the trip, I asked Harry to agree that after meeting with Marlon, if he wanted to acquire the book, his offer would not be less than $3.5 million. He agreed.

I told Marlon about the progress with Harry and Random House. The conversation halted there. Harry is married to Tina Brown, then editor of *Vanity Fair,* which had published what Marlon thought was a hateful article about Christian's trial. He was venomous about her. When he gets that kind of a fix on someone, Marlon is truly Don Corleone, the vendetta is in his eyes. I wanted to keep his focus on his book.

"I understand how you feel about that article, Mar, but Tina Brown would have nothing to do with your book."

"We don't know, bedroom bullshit, when they're there at night they'll talk about it."

"There's something else, good-news and bad-news department. Random House and *Vanity Fair* are both owned by the Newhouse family, so Harry and his wife are close corporately, too; that's the bad news. The good news is because the two publications are closely connected, they'll have to be hospital clean. We'd have an enforcing clause."

It didn't dent Marlon. "Anybody married to her has a weakness, likes being pussy-whipped. She's self-promoting and sinister."

"Those are strong judgments when you haven't met either of them. In your own interest it's a judgment you don't want to make too early. Maybe Tina Brown will turn out to be a reason you won't associate with Random House; we can deal with that later. Right now we've got a business opportunity, I'd like us to concentrate on that."

"I've watched her caught up in her own disgusting ego. Being in charge, being an image, she loves the idea she's boss, she can cut the nuts off the guys around her. Look at the photographs she's in everywhere, she wants to be more glamorous than the models, wants you to say how can anyone be so sexy and so smart at the same time—repugnant twat."

"Okay, I'll tell him not to come."

I've seen Marlon wreck so many deals, so many projects—everything is going the right way and suddenly he flings in some new condition. Then he won't budge from it.

The mistake people almost inevitably make when he gets into this mode is to try to hold things together. You have to walk. If that ends it, okay, it would have ended down the road anyway. I'd worked hard in New York to create a fine deal and he was wrecking something good for him, but it was clear what to do. If Random House was mentioned again, it would come from him, not from me.

"I'm hungry for catfish, want to come?" I said as I stood up, ready to leave.

"Who the hell eats catfish?

"Bonnie's father loves catfish." Bonnie was my second wife. "He's a great man, I'd trust him about anything, so when he said he'd take me down to a perfect little place on the Tennessee River, I was a believer. He was right, there's nothing quite like catfish."

"Next you'll tell me how good poi is. 'Want to bring some taro roots up to your house, Mar, dig a big hole in the back and bake them for three days. You won't be able to stand the smell and the neighbors will want you deported to Molokai, but we'll have some fine poi that'll stick to the roof of your mouth.' "

"No chance, I've tasted poi."

"So have I."

"Awful."

"It's like eating Hawaiian farts," Marlon said, but that doesn't mean you're not going to try to get me to believe how good poi is. Why do they call it catfish, those huge ugly whiskers sticking out from its mouth?"

"Southerners call it catfish because it jumps like a cat."

"You are so full of shit it's pitiful, that doesn't even get on the humor scale, let alone into funny."

"It does, it jumps off the plate onto your shoulder and hangs on like a cat."

I got up, went over to Marlon, and kissed him on the cheek.

"Where you going?" he said. "Driving to Palm Springs tonight?"

"Probably. See Georgie then head down." I was picking up my briefcase.

"Might as well tell that guy to come."

"Who?"

"Harry Evans. If he's got the gelt, let's talk to him. I'll smoke him out about his wife when he gets here."

"I don't want to bring him here dishonestly, Mar. Talk to him on the phone first if his wife's a problem, but if he comes, we've got to be ready to do business, you've got to be a good boy."

"I will."

He got up and walked me to the door. " 'Night, Georgie."

" 'Night, Mar. I'm your agent, trust me."

"Tired, Georgie, tired of being suspicious, tired of being tired. 'Night, kid, I love you."

"Love you, Mar." We hugged each other and I left.

The day before Harry arrived, I described him to Marlon in more detail: English, energetic, an admirer of Marlon's but not goony. Literary, used to be editor of the Sunday *London Times,* humorous, likable. I had a growing sense that this deal could work. There would be role-playing, we knew how to fall in with each other. It felt like a con, Newman and Redford in *The Sting.*

Marlon and I are always competing with each other; often the competition is an improvised joust, no point, no business, no profit, just the fun of competing. But when we work together and the green is on the table, we can be a strong combination. If we'd tried, we could have owned Kansas.

When I drove Harry up to Marlon's house for a before-dinner chat, I lent the upcoming meeting a formality. I was the Cardinal Camerlengo leading Harry to the inner temple where the rites would be performed.

In his living room the laird was scrubbed and smiling, at one with the world. Marlon welcomed Harry and sat him down. Marlon's humor shone, his curiosity went like a sea turtle deep into Harry's ocean. And Harry was pleased.

Like a master chef exhibiting the elements of the meal he was going to prepare, Marlon lifted the tops off his pots. In here is the raconteur, you see? Boom, the lid is back on. In here, well, a little mixing of aphorisms, a few quotes from Afghan Buddhists for accent, no? Boom, the lid. Here, some morsels of Keats and Shelley and two lightning insights about Kazan as a director for chewiness, yes? And over in this pot . . . glorious, wholesale, riveting bullshit.

Things went well. Harry enjoyed Marlon and did well in the conversation with him. In his sturdy English way he traded shots on an equal footing with Marlon. It was time for dinner.

"What kind of food do you feel like, Harry?" said Marlon, largesse from the owner of the estancia.

"Wherever you like to go, Marlon, whatever you like to eat, I'm easy." The upper gorillas approving of each other.

"I know what we'll do." Marlon snapped his fingers. "French sound good?"

"Lay on, Macduff." The nice riposte from Harry, not the plebeian mistake of, "*Lead* on, Macduff."

And I was the sly-eyed messenger who'd brought them together. I lingered behind on the way to the car in the hope that they might find greater closeness in the narrow compass of this single evening.

Marlon knew the restaurant's owner and spoke with him in French, the kind of French that makes you applaud it's so good. Not just the words, the casual perfection of the accent, the facial expressions, the one-up one-down eyebrows, the nasal snorts that say, "Piss on the rest of the world, we French know what is funny in the life."

After dinner, after we took Marlon home, Harry and I sat in the Bel Air Hotel bar. It was quarter to eleven when we arrived. The piano player was noodling " 'Deed I Do." New York types were scattered in other booths, the place was relaxed but alive. In our booth there was hushed excitement. Harry's perceptions of Marlon were elegiac and crisp. He talked of Marlon's uniqueness, his power, his curiosity, his learning, his sensitivity. I felt we were getting near the close.

"Harry," I said, "I think this autobiography, the view of cinema, politics, and women from Marlon's side of the eyeballs, could be not just a bestseller but something of lasting value in the history of the arts."

"I wouldn't disagree, it's quite possible."

We took time, rinsed the thought through our mouths as with an important wine, pushed it into our cheeks, breathed across its body.

"That three and a half million, I think you can see that's not the right figure, Harry," I offered.

"No, well, three and a half million is great deal of money, very few books get that much of an advance."

"Harry, I want to stop here. I don't want to demean you or Marlon or the book with a wrangle about dollars. You're in California, you've seen the man, what do you think the price should be?"

"I can go higher than the three and a half. And I think it's appropriate we do. I think I could go to four."

"Well, that's the right sentiment. But four is not going to get you the book."

"What? What in God's name are you thinking about? More?"

"I've already been offered four in New York. I've brought only one other publisher to meet Marlon and he's very much in the game. But you've spent a longer time with Marlon than anyone, you've really seen what the book can be. It's worth more than four. Isn't it?"

"The book could be a phenomenon, but at some point the risk becomes too great, you just have to leave it to somebody else to publish."

"At some point, all right. Let's find where that point is."

"We're very near it, George. Honestly. And don't forget, Marlon hasn't written one word. He's wonderful to have dinner with, but that isn't a guarantee he can write."

"It is a guarantee. If he just talks it into a microphone, people will be hearing things they've never heard, never imagined."

"George, I think . . . I'll go to four and a half and let's consider it done. You've got a marvelous deal for your client, and mind you, you have done an exceptional job for Marlon, I give you my honest opinion."

There was a long pause.

"I hope to God we have a deal," Harry said, astounded. "My God, what are you going to say, is there something more?"

"Harry . . . let me ask one question. If Marlon's book were

completely finished, if it lay right here on the table in front of you and you read it, and it was all the things you hoped it could be, everything we've discussed, it would be the talk of the book world . . . what would you pay for it?"

"We're going into the ozone, George. Only so many books can be sold on planet Earth, four and a half million is an extraordinary offer."

"It is an extraordinary offer. But let me tell you why I think Marlon's autobiography is worth more and why Random House is the one to publish it. When you've crossed from near the beginning of Marlon's life to now as I have, witnessed the triumphs, the explorations of the soul, seen the immense engine that drives him, one thing is clear: Marlon needs an editorial hand to bring out his humor, his sexuality. He needs to be guided back into that cold cave where he goes alone when he's anxious. If you get all that, it's a five-million-dollar book, Harry."

"Perhaps. If it had all that."

"It's there if Random House can mine it. You'll find out how good you are because the book can be everything we've said. And more."

There was a longish moment. Then Harry spoke quietly.

"All right, George, five million."

We shook hands and touched glasses. I'd made Marlon's deal.

The contract took months to get completed. I went over every detail, every piece of arithmetic, some aspects of Marlon's contract were unprecedented—the gross amount of the deal, the schedule of payments, his approvals in all areas.

It was shock and awe for Marlon that he was getting a five-million-dollar guarantee without having written a single word. We had a nice chat, we looked back on the night when he first proposed that I be his agent.

"You did something fantastic, Georgie. I thought you'd be the best for me, I really never imagined you'd do it this successfully. Well done, my boy."

I had told Harry Evans the truth; there is a book in Marlon valuable beyond dollars. Not in everything he would say—he would wax too long on the Indians, admonish you that America can produce everything except happy people, you'd have to thin that out. But the little forests where his soul has lain, the gossamer curiosity net he has laid across people, the gentle boy who lurks beneath the crust, in him is a report from a remarkale soul.

But to get this book would take a monumental effort because Marlon is the toughest old bull in the pasture. There he stands down in the corner watching you approach. And he is thinking, Here comes another who wants to know the inside of me. He turns around and lifts his tail and shows you his asshole. "Could this be what you've come for?" his big head asks as it turns to look at you. And your association with Marlon has begun.

11

No, sleep would not come this night. If it appeared at all, it would slip briefly in beside me, then it would leave and I would stay behind with wide, wondering eyes. I remem bered that once, when Marlon and I were mad at each other and not talking, I started thinking about the meaning of the word *friendship*, what makes a friendship, what are the friends obligated to do. I did some reading on the subject and found no consensus.

The dictionary defines *friend* as "A person one knows, likes and trusts." Pretty general; even the dictionary doesn't want to get specific.

La Rochefoucauld, in his *Maxims for Living*, says cynically: "In life it is not enough to have achieved great personal success, one's best friend must also have failed."

Emerson's view: "A friend may well be reckoned the masterpiece of nature."

Lord Byron: "I have had a thousand friends, they are like one's partners in the waltz of this world—not much remembered when the ball is over."

Thomas Jefferson: "Friendship is but another name for an alliance with the follies and misfortunes of others. Our own share of miseries is sufficient: why enter then as volunteers into those of another?"

Like the blind men trying to describe an elephant, each of these authors gave his subjective definition and experience of friendship. The closest description of the friendship between Marlon and me is, I think, Aristotle's. When he was asked, "What is a friend?" the philosopher replied, "A single soul dwelling in two bodies." At our best that is how it has been.

There is another element in being Marlon's friend. We live in a star culture and in that pantheon of gods are not only movie stars but sports stars, writer stars, teen stars, rock stars, lawyer stars, TV anchor stars, business stars, animal stars—dogs, mules, bears, dolphins. Ours is an undiscriminating totem pole, criminals and religious leaders claim equal space, John Gotti's head is the same size as Billy Graham's.

If there is a first among equals, it is the movie star. This figure, concocted of light and shadow, that moves in little squares in front of the projector at twenty-four frames per second, when he hates his enemy, when he loves his woman or his horse, this person brings an incandescence to our lives that no other figure or form can. When the movie actor achieves stardom, he becomes quasi-omniscient, we write to him not only to say how affected we have been by a performance, but to ask advice about raising a gay teenager or whether mutual funds are a better play than individual stocks. The queen mother of England wrote to Marlon to tell him how much one of his performances fortified her resolve in dealing with a personal problem.

We do not see the movie star as a being like ourselves, filled with pleasure at the emptying of his bowels. And he is not like us; he is worried that he is not first on his agent's client list, dreading to read his bad notices, stressed at not being certain whether he is loved for himself or his stardom, even by his wife and children. Or his best friend. Movie stardom wrenches the world around for everyone, maybe most jarringly for the star himself. If he makes three pictures in a row that lose money; who will he be then? Not who he is now, no longer enjoying "favored nation" status, being the center of attention, recipient of adoring stares. That person will vanish. Who remains? A character actor? One who appears frequently in whatever-happened-to columns? A real-estate broker? A suicide?

The public gives you support and strong shoulders when you, the incipient star, are on your way up. But then, when you are fixed in the firmament, with stunning swiftness, with breathtaking rapacity, your public and its flesh-eating troops, the media, make a remorseless assault on you, on your alcoholic father, your teen daughter, your failed romance with another star, there is never enough evisceration of you, there are never enough photographs of you scowling, looking fat, looking angry, hauled in on a DUI. There is no code of behavior that restrains pursuing paparazzi, anything and everything can be imputed to you—drug addiction, abuse of talent, abuse of wife, dyslexia, anorexia, loss of every cent you've made, and photographs to substantiate the imputations.

At this point you may have difficulty remembering what about you once seemed so appealing to people—and what now attracts so wholesale a debasement of you. I have seen this media lust in close-up when it was directed at Marlon. As it has been many times through the years.

This night Marlon is in need of help, support, an easing of his turmoil. It is my chance to be the parent once more, the father—there's that word again, *father.* Tonight it evokes the memory of the time I went to see my own father. That event captured Marlon's interest more than almost anything else has through the years of our friendship.

I was living in an English cottage above the Sunset Strip. Keeping house for me was a tall, over six-feet-two, rawboned German woman, Marta Sohnius. Very well schooled, very well-bred, she added a touch of Europe to life, she knew Swiss and German wines as well as French, she knew painting and fine fabrics.

Marlon stayed over frequently with one or another of his girlfriends and often there were vestiges of the lovemaking the next morning. But nothing disturbed Marta's old-world poise. After she'd made up the guest room, she might come to me with a bra or a pair of panties.

"Mr. Englund, what you vould like I should do with this?" A wisp of a smile and a flicker of merriment in her eyes.

"What is it?" I'd ask, looking at the garment with a straight face.

She'd smile conspiratorially. "*Ja,* maybe I launder and you giff back to Mr. Brando, he vill know what is."

Because of a flood in the canyon where she lived, my mother had come to stay with me. Her house had been substantially wrecked by a mud slide, and while it was being repaired she felt happy and secure with Marta and me.

I was going to Palm Springs one Friday night after dinner and would return on Sunday night. Monday I was leaving for New York. At dinner on that Friday, I told my mother I'd decided to stop in Detroit on the way back to L.A. and see Rip, my real father. She was startled.

"Why?" she said. "What made you even think of it?"

"I don't really know. It just hit me that the man who gave me life is alive. He and I ought to see each other."

"But why now?"

"There's no single reason. I'm thirty-six and this is the first time it's occurred to me."

"Do you really want to open something that could be very painful?"

"I don't know if I'll be opening anything, maybe it'll be nothing. It's time to see."

When I got back from Palm Springs, Marta had the table beautifully set and dinner was waiting. My mother and I sat down, graceful and easy, but from the beginning the conversation didn't flow.

"Anything wrong?" I asked.

"No, why?"

"Seems like there is."

"No, there's nothing." She smiled reassuringly.

We talked on, but that trace of something underneath stayed. I sat back and looked at her.

"Muth, what is it?"

"Nothing." A pleasant smile. "Why do you think there's something?"

"Because there is."

She stared at me. "I called Rip," she said.

I felt a bomb go off. "What?"

"I called Rip, I thought you—"

"You thought what—what the hell has this got to do with you?" I was almost shouting.

"I thought he might not want to see you."

"What he wants has nothing to do with it, I've decided to see him."

"I didn't want you to be hurt."

Everything she said made me wilder. "I'm not going to be hurt, if anybody's at risk it's him."

I had been telling this to Marlon and at this point he stopped me. "Why did you react so emotionally, what was going on, what were you thinking?"

"I don't know, Mar, I just erupted, I didn't plan it, I wasn't even ready for it."

"Okay, what happened then?"

It took a minute to get my voice quiet, I told him, till I could speak civilly.

"When did you last talk to Rip?" I asked my mother.

"A long time ago, George, more than thirty years."

"Thirty years . . . what did he say when you told him I was going to see him?"

"He was surprised, very surprised, he asked if it was certain you were coming. I told him you seemed absolutely certain."

We ate in silence, then she spoke again. "I'll tell you one thing, George; you'd recognize him anywhere, you look exactly like him."

"Did you know what he looked like?" Marlon asked. "Ever seen a picture of him?"

"No picture, nothing, he was a blank."

"And you still didn't know why you wanted to find him at that particular moment in your life?" Marlon asked.

"No, it was almost mystical; something moved me to go see him."

Marlon was intense, this was one of the purest of the moments we had shared while trying to understand our fathers and why they had so much force in our lives.

It was surprising how little I knew about Harold Austin Ripley. He came from Washington, D.C. His family went back to the American Revolution. My middle name is Howe, I'm named for General Howe and Lord Admiral Howe, who fought against General Washington in the battle for Long Island. Rip was an alcoholic; in his time they were called heavy drinkers. My mother was young when she married Rip and didn't understand his condition. He'd lie passed out on the sofa, and when his coworkers called from the office, she'd tell them he was ill.

I heard from my grandmother that when I was six months old, Rip arrived one night, deeply drunk, at our apartment in Washington. She seemed to remember the scene exactly as it happened. This is how I have pictured it.

"I'm taking the children away," Rip slobbered when he came in. My mother was five-four, Rip was six-two. He stood over her, boozed and hostile. She remonstrated with him, but he was hell-bent on getting the kids. He shoved her aside and started to the room where my sister and I slept.

"I'm taking the kids out of here," he said.

My mother got in front of him, protesting. He shoved her again and looked down at her. "Now get out of the way, Mabel."

"All right, Rip, just wait one second, okay?" She went to the kitchen, took a steel knife from the drawer, came back, walked up to him, and put the point of the blade to the left of his sternum, where his heart was.

"You're taking those kids over my dead body," she said. Her blue eyes were feral; she was flooded with adrenaline.

"Jesus."

That's what my grandmother told me Rip said. He was indignant; Mabel didn't understand about drinking and rage. You didn't take a knife out, you had to know the guy was heading into a massive hangover. You were supposed to know how to handle it. She didn't. It could have gotten worse, really bad, but my grandmother persuaded Rip to leave. He never came back.

The only other time I heard of Rip was when Ken Englund was adopting my sister, Patsy, and me. I was eleven. We had to go to court dressed in our best and the judge asked if we liked Ken and wanted him to be our father. Ken had been truly wonderful, we readily said yes. But I didn't know then what I was being asked. I had to sign documents that Rip had already signed approving the adoption. I was too timid to ask, even to phrase the question to myself: Why would he let his children become someone else's?

I told Marlon that if that awful night could be lived again, Rip roaring in drunk saying he was taking me away, I'd have gone with him. The fright of leaving my mother I'd manage somehow, she'd find me again. But if Rip went out the door, I'd never see him again. "Dad," I would have said, "take me with you, take care of me just till I grow up, and I promise I'll take care of you later on."

On the way back from New York I stopped in Detroit. Rip had become famous as director of a home for alcoholic priests called Guest House, in Pontiac, Michigan, outside Detroit.

It was February and very cold. I'd rented a car and stayed overnight at a hotel. The next morning I walked to the cathedral in the middle of the city; it was immense and somber and Gothic. I found the sexton setting chairs in a small chapel.

"Excuse me, do you happen to know Mr. Austin Ripley?"

"Who doesn't know Mr. Ripley."

"Good, do you know where I might find him?"

"Not here, you'll find him out at Guest House. They've got an office in town two blocks that way; you can come in and telephone them if you want."

"Thanks."

We went to his office. When I called, a woman answered.

"Is Mr. Ripley there, please?"

"Oh, you've just missed him, he's gone out to Guest House. You could call him there, but he won't arrive for half an hour or so."

"Maybe I'll just run out there."

"Do you have an appointment?"

"Not exactly. I think he knows I'm coming."

"You're not from around here, are you."

"No."

"It's a little tricky to find. We have maps if you want to come by, it's the Cadillac building. Maybe it would be a good idea to call out there and say you're coming."

"Probably would be. See you in a few minutes."

"Were your feelings changing as you got closer to seeing him?" Marlon asked when I recounted this part of the story.

"Yeah, I was changing, I could feel it, something big."

It was one of the tall office buildings. On the third floor the lettering on the window, that wavy glass you can't see through, said GUEST HOUSE. I went in. It was a small reception room; a pretty and buxom woman of thirty-eight or thirty-nine was sitting behind the desk. She looked good; she looked startled, too.

"You're . . . ?"

"Englund. I called just now."

"Oh, yes."

She swept me with her eyes. My mother's words came back: "You look exactly like him." The woman must have seen something of Rip in me. I wondered if she had anything to do with Rip; she seemed too attractive just to sit in this office.

"Do you have that map?" I asked.

"Yes, right here." She placed a pad on the front of her desk, I walked over. "Here's the street you take out of the city, it's the main street, you can see it out the window." She looked at me again. "Did you call Mr. Ripley?"

"Not yet."

"I think it would be a good idea."

"Probably I will."

That didn't lighten things; she wanted me to call him in front of her. She turned back to the pad and traced the route. I felt odd again. Why didn't I say who I was? I remembered that when my parents were divorcing, Rip had wanted an annulment and my mother wouldn't agree to it. She divorced him. He was married again—was he also having an affair with this woman? I didn't know how he could be married; in those days there was no such thing as divorce in the Catholic Church.

Why didn't I just say, "I'm his son, I've never seen him, he's never seen me, now I'm here"? I was ashamed to say it. He had never called me son.

"I think I must insist you call Mr. Ripley." The woman had put her hand over the pad, she was very disconcerted.

I reached down, took her hand off the pad, and tore off the map. I did it carefully, but the gesture was hostile, I was hostile. I felt dark and outside myself. I turned and left the office. Why couldn't it have been simple? Why couldn't that woman and I have been pleasant with each other? I was only going to see my father.

As I got to the edge of the city, there was less traffic. Cold Michigan winter, working people in heavy coats, galoshes, and scarfs. I felt wary, I was in an alien place. Ahead I saw a coffee shop with angled parking places in front. There was one vehicle parked, a police car. I turned in. I didn't drink coffee, but I went in. Two policemen were at the far end of the counter. I ordered a coffee. I took perfunctory sips and realized I'd stopped because the police were there, police kept order. That was quieting because inside me a turbine was winding up.

It was the old Scripps estate. Rip had started treating alcoholic priests in a farmhouse in Wisconsin when no bishop in the country would admit there was such a thing as an alcoholic priest. His work had brought him success and now he'd been given this huge facility. The estate was surrounded by a fieldstone wall. I turned into the large gateway; an older man in a black coat was walking along the drive. I stopped and rolled down my window.

"Can I help you?" he said with a smile and an Irish brogue.

"I'm looking for Mr. Ripley."

"I can take you there, it's enough of a walk I've done in the cold air." He stepped around and got in the passenger seat.

He was one of the fallen; I looked at his face and could see the broken veins around the nose from too much alcohol. We chatted as we wound up the long driveway to the main house. The courtyard was enormous, the house formal and imposing. Twenty of the bedrooms were done in the decor of different countries. All the building materials for each of the rooms, the fabrics and furniture, came from that country.

It was just on five o'clock, the last of the gray winter light was dying. Inside, the warmth, the tobacco smoke, the chatter of the forty priests made animated contrast to the outside chill.

"In that little room over there, the young man can tell ye," the older priest said.

It was an alcove off the living room. A fellow in his late twenties sat at a desk talking with the priests, answering their questions. I waited for a break, he looked to me.

"I'd like to see Mr. Ripley."

"You have an appointment?"

"No, but he knows I'm coming, I think he'll want to see me."

"He just got here and we're about to have dinner, it'll have to be tomorrow."

"I won't be here tomorrow."

"I don't know what to tell you, pal, it's not going to be tonight."

"Don't call me pal, my name is Englund, tell him I'm here."

"I don't have to tell him anything. I'm telling you something and you don't seem to get it, it's after hours, you should have made an appointment."

I leaned down to him, white and taut. "Tell him George Englund is here and I want to see him."

The guy could see the next thing would be me and him rolling on the floor. He was tough, he didn't want to back down, but I was unmistakably violent.

"Wait over there," he said.

I sat, a dark tangent to the orange circle of good fellowship. Quickly he was back, very changed.

"Mr. Ripley asked me to show you to the library."

He led me to a magnificent room, antique editions, first editions, there were millions of dollars in those volumes. I picked a chair and waited. I noticed I'd sat where I'd see the man enter before he saw me.

My father walked in.

She's crazy, I don't look anything like him, is what I thought. I stood up.

He was attractive, tall, not quite as tall as I, bald, good energy, the right person to be head of this place. I was on my feet, I didn't know what to call him.

"I'm George." We shook hands. "I know my mother called."

"She did, yes."

"I didn't ask her to, I didn't want her to say I was coming, I didn't want you to be worried."

"Well, it was a surprise . . . yes, I was a little concerned, I didn't know what prompted . . ."

"I don't know myself why I decided to come. It wasn't to upset your life, that wasn't in my mind."

He was relieved, he had been worried. Why not? He gets a

message that a thirty-six-year-old guy who's his son is coming, he doesn't know who'll show up. Maybe somebody really pissed off, somebody nuts, somebody who'll blackmail him—give me money or I'll blow your fucking lies about not having kids all the way back to the Vatican.

"It's good to see what a fine young man you've turned out to be, George," my father said.

Once again Marlon stopped me. "He walks into the room, you see him, this man who's your father, what exactly did you feel, can you tell me that?"

"I was so much in the minute, Mar, watching him, not sure what I was going to say. Thoughts didn't crystallize till later."

"I've read about the work you do," I said to my father. I had heard how he'd gone into the worst places, homes for derelicts, to find some of these priests, one of them he found in the top bunk of a flophouse in Trenton.

"Well, we're trying, we're getting better at it. Let me show you some of the place."

He took me first to the chapel. In it was the largest organ I have ever seen. He went to the font, put his fingers in the holy water, made the sign of the cross. How strange. Who was this man cloaked in Catholic ritual? He was one of the Gentiles my grandmother warned me not to play with when I was a boy.

"I'm not Catholic," I said.

"No, of course, I understand, it's just, I've done this all my life . . ." We left the chapel.

Near the dining room he introduced me to three priests talking together. "I'd like you to meet Mr. Englund, he's joining us for dinner."

We shook hands, I said I was glad to meet them, we exchanged pleasantries. As we left the group, the oldest turned to the other two.

"What did he say his name was?"

"England, was that it?"

"Looks just like Rip, doesn't he?" the older priest said.

I wondered how Rip would handle the inquiries about me when I was gone.

We sat alone in an alcove of the dining room. He told me more about Guest House, I told him a little about my life, about the movie industry. Two completely different spheres. As we talked I went suddenly dry; I stared at him. I was exactly like him. The way he cleared his throat, chose his words, listened, smiled, explained. I had never seen him before, but we were mirrors of each other. It was alarming, staggering, sad.

After dinner we went upstairs to his room. He was a man of another era, he smoked Raleigh cigarettes. He told me he was married to a woman who had saved his life, had stood by him during his hard climb out of alcoholism, he'd been sober now for nineteen years. I asked how he could be married again. Through a rarely granted dispensation called the Pauline privilege, he said. Saint Paul had allowed two of the faithful to be married after one had been divorced under the condition they live as brother and sister. The Vatican granted Rip this privilege.

Our conversation was interesting but not personal, we had not touched the deep chords, the kind of chords that would be played on that organ in the chapel. They had to be there in both of us. Father and son in the same room for the first time in their lives; there were tidal emotions. But they had stayed out of sight so long they would not surface easily. I decided what I'd call him.

"Rip, it's getting late and I know you rise early in this place, so I'll take off. Just one last thing. I said when I got here I didn't know why I'd come. And I didn't. Now I think I do. It's this, Rip . . ." I felt a surge up my gut. "I have three kids. I'm not the best father in the world, I get it wrong, I'm away too often, I'm too much of a disciplinarian sometimes, but one thing is for sure. If there was ever something wrong with any of my kids, if they needed me, no power on earth could keep me away, you'd have to kill me to stop me. My question is"—an air bag inflated and pressed on my larynx—"how could you have had Patsy and me all those years and never known if we needed you, if we were hungry, if we were alive? We were yours, Rip . . ."

The emotion was so much bigger than the little words that had to carry it—it was planet size. He'd had a son and I'd had a father. What we might have shared was facing us; how do you begin talking about that? The subway that had run under my whole life roared up to the elevated tracks.

"George . . . I'm an alcoholic, a recovering alcoholic, we say. I was underwater for eighteen years, no good to anybody. But I can tell you this . . . in all those years not one day went by that you and Patsy were not in my heart and in my prayers."

Two emotions collided in me. One, gratitude; I had been in his prayers, he had cared about me. The other was a nuclear fireball. You weak, lying son of a bitch, anybody can make a phone call, fuck how much you drank, get up off the floor and call. How's my kid, I love you, son. I know, Dad, I love you, too, it's great to hear your voice. I wanted to die. I wanted to kill somebody, him and me.

We stood a long time, caught in the miracle of how intimately we were tied and what strangers we were. We walked downstairs and out to my car and I thought of all the basketball games I'd played, all the tennis matches. I'd done them for him, I knew that now, won for him, went through the heat of adolescence bringing girls home for him to approve of. I couldn't think in a straight line, but one thought distilled.

It wasn't Rip I was looking for, not somebody who would have me only in his prayers, not this man who had a sector in him so empty he could not say I was his son. Those priests were his children, they received his care and attention. I thought of Wordsworth's lines about "shades of the prison-house" closing upon "the growing boy" and how "the child is father of the man."

It was very cold, I had an overcoat on and Rip was in just a suit. I gave him a hug, held him in my arms. I'd come to this place to find something and I had—a well-intentioned man. But not my father, not him of the manly soul I longed for. I looked into Rip's face; he had broken veins, too.

I said I'd like to see him again, but I understood it would be difficult to explain a grown son; he could call if it ever felt right.

Rip died eight years later. He never did call. He left five thousand dollars each to Patsy and me. Patsy and I gave the money to our mother.

The story was just a story, I said to Marlon. I didn't feel any deep emotion as I was telling it to him. Yet in the middle I was halted. A few tears came, then I went on. But the hiccuping of crying worked in my windpipe.

"I know it seems I'm emotional, but I'm really not feeling anything, Mar. I saw my father, that's all, I found him and he was . . ."

The torrent started, the crying shook me.

Marlon waited. "You're not crying because you found him, it's because you didn't find him, Georgie. You're not going to find him, not the guy you're looking for. You'll find some substitutes. Like me. I'll be proud of you, Georgie."

A deep moment. Atheist Marlon exploring with me the mystery of God's ways.

I had to put my mind on other things or this night would turn into a seventeenth-century event at Bedlam. I came back to the *Lying for a Living—Master Class* DVD. On it Marlon wanted me to talk about him as an actor and as a man. I'd thought about it and decided what I'd say first is that Marlon is unrivaled by anyone I know or ever heard of at one thing, controlling his world. If he had political ambitions, he might govern a nation or be a grand ayatollah. He is not interested in that sort of control; his attention is on dominating and manipulating the elements in the immediate sphere of his life.

Marlon uses his acting genius only secondarily as a profession; its major employment is for gaining and maintaining control.

Looking at him only as an actor, he dominates the twentieth century the way Picasso dominates painting. Other actors were excellent and performed with beauty and riveted audiences with their skills. There were fine schools of acting and fine teachers, the Group Theater, the Royal Academy of Dramatic Art, the Juilliard, Sanford Meisner, Stella Adler. But, like Apollo, Marlon rode his chariot above all these fiefdoms. Actors, absorbed in their traditions and orthodoxies, looked up to see a new king. And he was so young, so primitive, so imperial.

Before Marlon, during rehearsals of plays, the most common mantra from the director was, "That's good, everybody, but we've got to pick up our cues, eliminate the dead spaces, and pull these scenes together." Marlon reversed that concept. When another actor addressed him in a scene, instead of hearing his cue and responding, he would study the actor and simultaneously seem to be involved in an inner dialogue about some mysterious other conflict. When the moment struck him he would respond. He did not pick up his cues.

With the advent of Marlon, pretty much all other views of acting went slack and actors herded around and tried to be like Marlon Brando. He didn't read his lines, he didn't memorize his lines, he didn't start with lines. He started with who he was and what he was feeling. He was open to the moment, to the look, the behavior, the certainty or lack of it in the actors with him. He didn't come to rehearsal with an organized plan the way Olivier did, he listened and watched and then he knew what he wanted to do. There were no rules for him, in acting or in life. Everything was open to observation, assimilation, and use.

Never mind the questionable choices Marlon made later in life, the way it seemed to some that he frittered away his magnificent talents. Which artist has walked a straight and sensible road his whole life? When he was at his best, Marlon was the best.

The leprechauns in my mind have jumped around again and brought me to a wholly other precinct of activities with Marlon.

12

In the sixties, Marlon's and my paths had a variety of intersections with the paths of the Kennedy family. Partly because of Marlon's stardom, partly because we'd made *The Ugly American,* which had been important to the Kennedys, partly because we all wanted to be part of the Kennedy action.

President Kennedy inaugurated a fund-raising vehicle called the President's Club. When he came to your city you were invited to a President's Club dinner at a thousand dollars per seat. There were ten tables, eleven seats at each table. During the meal the president sat in the empty chair at each table for fifteen minutes, chatted with everyone, and moved on. It was a nifty idea, sort of like a private audience with the pope, which usually means you and fifteen others.

Marlon and I went to the President's Club dinner at the Beverly Hilton together. We were seated at different tables. I

knew only two of the people with whom I was sitting. The president came to our table about halfway through the meal.

"Evening, everybody, anything I can get for you?" he began. There was appreciative laughter. Then quiet. One of those silences began that startles you with its length, then you become fearful, will it ever end, how will it end? Everyone seemed frozen, not wanting even to clear his throat or hit the plate with a fork.

Since I'd met the president before, I said, "Good evening, Mr. President, George Englund . . ."

"Yes, George, I remember."

"It's great sharing the meal with you, but it's too bad you have to work when you're out here in California."

He said, "I'm so happy to be out of Washington that this seems like fun." His candor was startling; you don't think that a president suffers in Washington, that he has a downright thirst sometimes for reaffirmation from the faithful.

"So what do we want to talk about?" he said.

That opened the door and the whole table entered, the talk was lively till he left.

After dinner, Gene Kelly; Pat and Peter Lawford; Red Fahey, secretary of the navy and an old friend of Kennedys; and Marlon and I went up to the presidential suite for the real dinner. It was catered by Jean Leon, owner of La Scala, a favorite restaurant of the Kennedys. Marlon and I were the first to arrive, and when the Secret Service ushered us into the large living room, a female voice rang out.

"Oh hi!" She was talking to me. "I know you." She was an attractive blonde, thirtyish, sitting on the sofa all alone.

She seemed familiar, but I couldn't recall where I'd seen her before.

"We met in Palm Springs with Jimmy Van Heusen, remember?"

That brought it all back. Jimmy Van Heusen was a dedicated employer of good-looking hookers. I had been at a dinner in Palm Springs that Jimmy had hosted, I'd come with Sammy Cahn, Van Heusen's songwriting partner. That's where this young lady and I met. She was witty, forthright, and sexual with a slightly used look.

The president and the others arrived; from the first the feeling was familylike. You could see that's what Kennedy wanted, what he enjoyed, the group gathered, the flowing bowl, friends and family.

Gene Kelly was a feisty guy with great humor, and Irish. He was never more Irish than this night when to be Irish was to be specially connected. Gene bubbled with the kind of light insults the Kennedys liked. There was also in Gene something you don't see a lot of, softness and respect. He was with the president of the United States, that meant a great deal to him.

The whiskey flowed and the voices rose and everybody got his oar in. But Marlon was the star, mysterious Marlon was the one the Kennedys focused on. I've been in every sort of company with Marlon, with presidents and prime ministers, truck drivers and telephone operators; he is the cynosure. The president led with a typical Kennedy needle.

"Marlon, have you gained weight? Looks like you put on a few."

"Nary an ounce." Marlon smiled through his mouthful of pasta.

"Then the CIA sent up some wrong information." The president grinned.

"And I'll bare-knuckle fight the man who says I have."

Marlon smote the table. "I'll bet you I weigh less than you do, Mr. President."

Party stuff, cooking up a conflict.

"You going to tell the president of the United States he's fatter than that?" Kennedy said, mock indignation.

Laughter from the rest of us.

"I'm not saying it, I'm guaranteeing it, where's a scale?"

The large helping of pasta still had not cleared Marlon's trachea; his words were muffled.

"Come on." The president was out of his chair and heading to the bathroom. The rest of us followed. He and Marlon squeezed next to the scale.

"You first, Mr. President."

"Marlon, you're with friends. Don't be shy, get on that scale and face the music," replied the president.

With urging from us, Marlon stepped onto the scale then set his fingertips on the tile trim to lift some of his weight.

"Marlon, what a horrible cheat," Pat Lawford said. "Take your hands off the wall."

Marlon laughed and took his hands down. He weighed 187 pounds. Kennedy showed his empty hands as he stepped onto the scale. He weighed 176.

"Get some food in this man," Marlon said as we headed back to the living room. "You can't lead a country at a hundred and seventy-six pounds."

The party moved through the gears—rising laughter, our heads cranked toward one another. I've read that laughter is the distinguishing trait of man, the one attribute that separates him from all others in the animal kingdom. If it is a distinguishing trait, it's probably a necessary one, it seemed necessary that night. The president was taking off for Asia in the morning and this revelry seemed to be his food for the trail; he wanted to work through its pleasure then lie down.

I got up to go to the bathroom and the president said, "In there, George, it's closer."

I went into the bedroom of the president's suite and crossed to the bathroom on the other side. His bed was turned down and his white silk pajamas were laid carefully where the sheet was folded. While I was in the bathroom I thought about this night I was part of. The quiet formality of the dinner downstairs, then the frat-house shoving and horse-play up here. The surprising sense of trust; Pat Lawford was the only actual family member present, but we were all family. There was trust that whatever went on, we knew it was private.

I'd read a book called *Conversations with Stalin* by Milo-van Djilas, an up-and-coming Yugoslav Communist who was brought to the Kremlin to meet Stalin. He described the vodka-driven eating binges at Stalin's dacha outside Moscow, his dismay at how Stalin toyed with his subordinates during the gastronomical orgy, manipulated, hinted at plots they might be hatching. Always pushing, always probing, setting one against the other during the relentless drinking and eating. With all the vodka consumption, Djilas said, there was no gaiety, no festivity. Stalin could—he had before and he would again—have any of them killed at will. I contrasted what Djilas described with the quality of this evening.

As I went back through the bedroom, I noticed a box of cigars on the night table. Across the top it read MADE IN HAVANA. Relations between the U.S. and Cuba at that time were antagonistic and angry. The Bay of Pigs fiasco was still fresh in the national mind; all travel, all trade with Cuba was curtailed. This was the official state of things—but then there were the real truths. First truth: In all this world, the finest cigars are produced in Cuba. Second truth: JFK loved good cigars. Third truth: Therefore, whatever the veerings of politics, into President Kennedy's possession would somehow come Cuban cigars. I wondered how many of those Made in Havana Davidoffs Kennedy smoked during the face-off with Khrushchev as the Soviet missiles were being put into Cuba.

"Mr. President, how much is it worth for me not to tell I saw those Cuban cigars on the night table?" I said, returning.

He laughed. "No, those are pre-embargo cigars, George, been in the family for years."

We laughed with him. Whatever would make the president happy we wanted him to have; we liked him, we liked the group we were part of. I run into Red Fahey every so often and the brightness of that evening remains for both of us.

We all left together, all except the blonde; she stayed. And that was fine, too; whatever would add to John Kennedy's pleasure or abet him in his mission he should have. Send him victorious, happy, and glorious . . . we are proud of him.

One of the fresh ideas of the Kennedy administration was the Peace Corps. It seemed to be a good subject for a movie. Universal liked the idea and I got Bud Burdick, coauthor of *The Ugly American,* to write the original story. We went to Washington to do our research.

We met Sargent Shriver, director of the Peace Corps, and quickly Sarge and I became friends. He was also executive director of the Kennedy Foundation, which does research on mental retardation. Sarge told me the Kennedy Foundation was going to put on its first annual awards dinner later that year. It would be a true gala; President Kennedy and the prime minister of Canada would be the guests of honor. Awards would be presented for research in the field of mental retardation.

A couple of days later Sarge said, "Why don't you give me some help on that dinner, you know how to do these things." I said I would. We met in New York, the event would be at the Americana Hotel. I could see what needed to be done and it was a lot. That night Sarge asked me to take charge of the event.

I was directing a picture at MGM. I'd finish work on Friday, take the red-eye to New York, work the weekend on the gala, and take the red-eye back Sunday night. The show grew; pretty soon we had a monster roster of stars and it was decided we should televise the event.

Two weeks before the Kennedy Foundation dinner was to take place, the president was assassinated. The country went into turmoil; the dinner, of course, was canceled.

Six weeks after the assassination, the Kennedy family was trying to decide what to do about the dinner. They asked me to come back for a meeting to help. Eunice Shriver, Jean Smith, and Bobby Kennedy and I met in the attorney general's office.

The decision was to reschedule the dinner for March 1964. President Johnson would be the guest of honor. I started the preparations again.

During the time of putting on the dinner, I had met Lee Radziwill, Jackie's sister. I was separated from Cloris and Lee and I spent a great deal of time together.

One weekend Marlon and I were in New York. Lee was in Washington visiting Jackie, who was still in seclusion. Averell Harriman had lent Jackie his house, and after the rigors of the assassination and the funeral, she had retired there to be away from public view. I called Lee to check in.

"Why don't you come down to Washington and have a drink with us," she said. "Jackie's been alone for weeks, she could really use some cheering up."

"I'd love to, but I'm catching the plane to L.A. in a couple of hours. I've got appointments tomorrow."

"You can have appointments anytime. Come down and you can go on to L.A. in the morning."

"Marlon's with me, he's got to get back, too."

"Bring him. Jackie can't go out, but we can have a cocktail with her, then the three of us can go to dinner."

"Hold on."

I gave Marlon the rundown, the decision didn't take long.

"What's the address?"

There were Secret Service inside and outside the Harriman house. We felt like college boys calling on our dates. We were shown into the living room and there were two of America's prettiest people. Jackie and Lee rose to greet us.

I gave Lee a cheek kiss and turned to introduce Marlon. It was nutty etiquette; Jackie and Marlon were probably the two best-known people in America. "Marlon, may I introduce . . ." Jackie stepped toward him.

"Hello, Marlon." She held out her hand, vivacious.

"Jackie, good to meet you."

"Jackie, this is George," said Lee.

"I've heard so much about you from Lee, George. I want to know how much of it is true."

"I can tell you, I'm the expert on that," Marlon said.

"Save it for later," Lee said. "We'll compare notes."

"Well, let's sit down." Jackie moved back to her chair. "It's so good of you both to change plans and come and comfort two sad sisters."

She had those wide eyes that seemed to say, "I know you've got something wonderful to tell me." I was struck by her speech; in person, that way her voice went up and down the scale seemed more pronounced.

We started drinking martinis, the great social lubricator. It was a good idea because we were all aware of how close we still were to the tragic event.

Marlon was good, he extended himself, he was gracious and funny. I watched Jackie, she was tickled to be in this light-hearted company. Lee, too; she hadn't met Marlon before, and like the rest of the world, she was impressed.

It was bedtime for Caroline and John John, as he was then called, so Jackie took us upstairs to be introduced and to say good night. The children were so young and so seemingly brave. Jackie introduced us and Caroline and John John said their how-do-you-dos with affecting good manners.

Not even the high drama of President Kennedy's funeral so hauntingly brought home to me the immensity of this family's loss as that moment with the children. These three now and forever would live without that dynamic, handsome husband and father.

When we went back downstairs we had to revive the party mood. But it was so important to have this evening be a happy one that we worked it back quickly. By the time we were on the third martini, the room was getting distorted to me.

"Jackie," I said, "I'm seeing three of you—all beautiful—

but I've got to get something to eat. I know you can't go out, if you want we'll send something back for you . . ."

"It is getting late; gosh, it's flown by so quickly," she said. "You know what, I'm having such a good time, I'd love to go out to dinner, the four of us."

Fine. Where. I'd eaten at the Jockey Club a number of times and sort of knew the owner. I could ask him to give us a private corner.

"The Jockey Club sounds good," Jackie said. I called.

"This is Mr. Englund, René . . ."

"George, good, coming in?"

"Yes. I want to bring Mrs. Jackie Kennedy and Marlon Brando."

"Me, too. I'd like also Charles de Gaulle, can you bring him as well?"

"No, but Princess Radziwill will be with us."

"This is true?"

"We need a table by ourselves and don't mention anything to the press; we have to keep them away. We'd like this to be a lovely dinner with no intrusions."

"Leave everything to me. You come now?"

"Fifteen minutes."

There was sizable commotion when Jackie told the Secret Service she was going out. They have to plan routes ahead of time and secure the premises that will be visited. But she was definitely going. A lot of crackling on the walkie-talkies and we were into a limo, one Secret Service agent driving, a second in the passenger seat. Another sedan followed.

René, cordial but not effusive, ushered us to our table in the back corner. The table was private, but getting to it meant a walk down the center aisle of the restaurant.

No one was expecting to see Jacqueline Kennedy out at a restaurant. Let alone with Marlon Brando. Eyes bugged, smiles froze, balls of veal stuck in cheeks. Fragments of sotto voce phrases . . . "my God" . . . "how do they know each other?" The diners knew they shouldn't stare, but this was a once-in-a-lifetime sight, Jackie Kennedy with Marlon Brando, her first time out since the assassination.

We ordered and the captain said he'd have the meal quickly. But just as the appetizers were arriving, René ran to our table. "The press arrived outside; if you don't want to be seen, we have to run out through the kitchen. I can take you in my car, but we must go this second."

We were out of our seats and hightailing it to the kitchen. If the press got pictures, the wildest speculation would start, and Jackie could kiss dignified widowhood good-bye. We went like fugitives into the kitchen amid the chefs and servers. The chopping, the barking of orders, the stacking of dishes stopped, the mouths formed in the shape of Os.

The Secret Service agents in the foyer caught the last glimpse of us heading toward the kitchen. Where was Mrs. Kennedy going? They'd stretched the rules by bringing her to the restaurant; now this.

René's car was a two-door vehicle, very crowded with the five of us in it. René sped away with his lights off. It was a stunt ride through Washington, our bones sticking into one another. At the Harriman house he squealed to a stop, we thanked him and ran out. The limo and the Secret Service sedan pulled in behind. There were superserious faces on the men in those cars; this little caper had been no joke to them.

Back inside, we were immediately reminded that the reason we'd left the house in the first place was to get something to eat; we hadn't and hunger was still with us. Marlon said he'd make omelets. Lee said she'd show him where the kitchen was; they left together. Jackie and I sat back and talked; we chuckled about our little adventure.

"I'm glad we didn't have to face the press," she said, "but it was fun, wasn't it?" She said again how glad she was Marlon and I had come; it was the perfect antidote to the somber days she'd been living.

"You forget how good it is just to laugh . . . I don't think I've imagined myself laughing since Jack died."

It was almost as if she'd tripped a switch. She paused, her thoughts went elsewhere.

"I didn't want to go to Dallas," she said. "I didn't want Jack to go, I thought the whole idea of Texas was wrong."

I remember so well her expression, her eyes luminous in recall.

"We landed in Dallas and taxied over to the parking place. They moved the stairs up outside, then the door was opened. Jack and I started down . . . the first thing I saw at the bottom of the stairs was the whole reason I didn't want to be in Texas, a symbol of everything I detested, one of those redneck police officers, a huge man wearing dark glasses."

I sat quietly, tethered to her words.

"The crowds were larger, more people than we expected, it was sunny, and they were friendly. We'd heard there might be anger on the route, demonstrations from right-wing groups, but we didn't see any. Mrs. Connolly said, 'You can't say Texas doesn't love you, Mr. President.' It didn't make me feel any better, and every time I looked at the motorcade, there was that same policeman on his motorcycle."

She paused, her eyes searching again.

"I didn't hear the gunshot . . . we suddenly slowed and I turned to see what was happening . . . there was Jack holding a piece of his head in his hand." Her hand was up in front of her forehead.

"It was hysteria from then to the hospital, everyone shouting—when we got there, they took Jack into the emergency operating room and closed the door. I wasn't allowed in, I was off to the side. I stood against the wall, people streaming around. I don't know how long I stood there, but I saw that same redneck policeman come out of the operating area. He looked around, and when he saw me he walked over. I couldn't imagine what this man wanted or what he was going to say to me. He took off his hat, then he said, 'Mrs. Kennedy.' I was surprised, I hadn't heard him speak before, his voice was kind, I didn't expect that. Tears started out of his eyes and he had trouble saying what he wanted to say. 'They didn't save him . . . the president is dead.' That's who told me, the symbol of everything awful. I knew it was possible someone would say those words, but I couldn't take them inside me. Then, in the most tender way, that redneck policeman put his arms around me and held me and I held on to his strength. Both of us were crying."

She was crying as she told me, so was I.

Marlon and Lee came back with the omelets. They could see the change of mood, but we all settled into eating what they had prepared, no explanations had to be given for any emotions that night. It seemed to me Jackie must never have recited the events of that day out loud before, her voice was spun glass as she talked.

There's no explaining the connection between thoughts in

a sleepless night; there's no logic, no sequence. Suddenly, inexplicably, into my mind came this one.

I was in Europe when Marlon's father died. A day after I came back to California, I went up to the house to pick Marlon up for dinner. But we started drinking whiskey and kept at it. We began to talk about his father and Marlon brought out the urn that held his father's ashes. He poured some of them onto the table between us. He poked through them. I didn't detect either sadness or a sense of loss. The fact that his father was dead hadn't diluted Marlon's anger at him.

As the whiskeys warmed us, we ruminated about the cremation process. At what temperature do they cremate bodies? How is it that every body burns down to just enough ashes to fit into these twenty-dollar urns? If you paid more could you get a bigger pile of ashes? With more bits of bone? Could the ashes be dried and compressed like jerky? Or formed into something practical, a toilet-paper roller perhaps. We were improvising all the possibilities.

Marlon put the ashes back in the urn and took it outside with us. We weaved over the lawn talking about Senior, shouting about him and what he had meant to Marlon. Then Marlon held his arms out and started twirling, he turned the urn upside down. And the ashes of his father were taken by the night wind and spread across his son's yard.

13

After the deal with Random House for Marlon's autobiography was finalized, but long before the book was actually written, Marlon asked me to take on another project for him. He had always wanted to keep Tetiaroa private for himself, but the cost of developing the place had increased over the years and maintenance of the atoll had become a financial drain. Some source of revenue was needed.

He had considered a number of ventures, from oyster farming to using the gradient temperatures of seawater as a source of power, but none of these had worked out. Any kind of industry was prohibited by his own edict and by Tahitian environmental policy. Thus the idea of a small and exclusive hotel on the atoll was born.

For a fee, day tours from Tahiti and Moorea were allowed to visit the atoll on an irregular schedule and sometimes members of the group stayed overnight. A large central area

housed the offices and the kitchen. Homemade meals were
served.

But this business was neither fish nor fowl. Marlon no
longer had his complete privacy—though his area of the
island was off-limits to visitors—nor was he gaining sufficient
income to make progress against his overhead costs. The
operation sputtered along; sometimes his former girlfriend
Reiko managed it, sometimes his wife Tarita. In the latter
years Marlon imported a series of professional managers.

Once before Marlon had considered building a hotel. He
tried to interest Japanese companies in the project, he thought
Tetiaroa could be an exclusive vacation place for wealthy
Japanese businessmen.

My guess is that plan didn't work because underneath it all
Marlon didn't want a Japanese-financed hotel and he didn't
want partners. What he wanted was the money with no real
commitment on his part, that was the thing to accomplish.
He put different lures on his hook, he would suggest being an
advocate for a large Japanese company, he'd make a documentary showing how its products were gloriously employed
in his environmental projects. But these were hasty sketches,
he didn't think them out.

Marlon believed that no one saw through these vaporous
proposals. He was convinced that these businessmen from the
Far and Middle East could be euchred into putting a large bit
of money into his plan solely because they'd be associated
with Marlon Brando.

When that format didn't work, Marlon came at it another
way. He would suggest a deal with the Japanese or the Saudi
Arabians in which he would star in a picture. They were to
finance the film, often, in the Arab case, to be about a cultural

hero like Saladin, and pay his guarantee—three million—up front. If Marlon could get his hands on that three million, there would be a new Ming dynasty in China before he'd make the movie.

The size of the Random House deal mesmerized Marlon, I think, and he believed I could make such deals work anywhere. Simultaneous with the hotel venture he proposed that I run another business.

"The rainwater in the mountains of Tahiti is the purest in the world. I want to bottle it and call it Marlon Brando's Tahiti Rainwater. We put some big capture tanks up in the mountains then flow it down to a bottling plant. We can sell it to Nestlé's, they own Perrier, it's a natural."

Vintage Marlon. An innovative idea though a bit outré, a lovely description of it, then a business plan made out of toilet plungers and the wheels off a '67 Volkswagen.

"Sell it the way you sold the book," he said.

"This is completely different, Mar. There isn't some mouth breather at the front desk I can gull into buying rainwater because it's got your name on it. Bottled water is Nestlé's business; we'd have to prove that Tahiti rainwater actually is the purest water on the planet."

"I'm having that done right now, the chemical analysis is being completed."

"Where?"

"These guys at the university at, um, over there, they'll have it ready and I'll show it to you within two weeks."

"Okay. Let's let it go till then."

"George, you're not taking this seriously. Bottled water is a four-billion-dollar-a-year business, I know we could have twenty-five percent of it."

"Mar, you don't go to supermarkets, there's one entire aisle of bottled water. It's a tremendously competitive field."

"None of that has my name on it. Think about that world market, we can get a huge piece of it, we can be rich."

"How do we get rich?"

"I'll give you two and a half percent."

"Of what?"

"Of the business."

"And you get ninety-seven and a half percent."

"Yeah, it's my idea."

"It's your idea, but I'd be doing all the work."

"But it's my name on it."

"Yes, it's your name."

"It's a good deal, it's a real good deal."

Where did he get two and a half percent? Why did he cling to it?

"Mar, let's let this go for a minute, tell me a little more about the hotel."

The hotel in Marlon's mind was to be small, luxurious, and built whenever possible of materials from the atoll. He described multiple uses of coral, how fresh water would be produced.

Marlon studies, he reads for hours, and when he tells you of the atoll's origins, its age and ecosphere, the lagoon's salinity, the amount of marine life it supports, you are impressed. Knowledge of almost any kind fascinates him and he carries its lure to you.

I said the idea of the hotel seemed good, I'd have a crack at putting it together. We didn't discuss the deal between us, another mistake on my part. I am the one with business experience, I should have protected both of us with a document.

I first called my friend Bill Kimpton in San Francisco. His extremely successful hotels are mostly in San Francisco, with new additions sprouting in Los Angeles, Portland, and Seattle. Smart purchasing and superb management are the hallmarks of Kimpton hotels. Bill is an old and close friend; I told him what Marlon wanted to do.

"It sounds tough and it's not for me, George. I've got my operation, that's what I know, you need somebody who specializes in this kind of very exclusive place. There aren't many and building it on an atoll with that fragile ecostructure makes it even harder. There's one guy I'd recommend, I think he'd be right for you, Adrian Zeccha."

Adrian Zeccha is one of the founders of Regent Hotels, the prized possession of which is the Regent in Hong Kong. Adrian, who is Indonesian, lives in Bali and has his headquarters in Hong Kong. By phone I described the project to him. He knew all about Marlon's atoll and was interested. He had just bought the Bora Bora hotel, not too far from Tetiaroa; remodeling was about to begin. He'd like to have a hotel on an atoll to go with the one on the island.

We made a date to meet in Los Angeles. I picked him up at the Beverly Wilshire Hotel and we went to dinner. Impeccably dressed in the English style, he was a man of the world, easy with his knowledge, and had been everywhere you'd been but didn't flaunt it. We knew a number of the same people.

He asked if I'd seen his hotel Amanpuri on the island of Pukhet, off the coast of Thailand. I had not, but I'd heard tales of its splendor and of his other hotels on Bali.

Each of his hotels has approximately forty bungalows, the cost to stay is upward of $750 per night. Anything and everything the guest wants for life, for sport, for relaxation is there.

Guests sign for nothing, whatever they order is put on the bill, which is forwarded to the client's office; there is no checking out. He invited Marlon and me to come to Pukhet and see his way of doing things.

After dinner I called Marlon and told him I thought Zeccha was an excellent candidate to be his partner on Tetiaroa.

"We'll be at your house for lunch at twelve-thirty, so don't be down buying new eels. Zeccha changed his itinerary for this meeting."

"Georgie, never fear, Marlon's here."

"Okay. Tomorrow, lunch," I said emphatically.

"Great, see you at five."

"Yeah, right."

Adrian and I came up to Marlon's house by limousine. There is a pillar in front of the large black gates with two buttons on it, one to Jack Nicholson's house, the other to Marlon's. When you push the button a voice asks you to identify yourself. Marlon has a TV camera focused where the car stops so he can see whatever's going on.

I got out of the limousine and pushed Marlon's button. Silence. A moment, then I pushed again. It was getting dark inside my stomach, this was too familiar. Marlon might have decided to avoid the meeting. I remembered the times I had helped him evade others, watched their bewilderment on the monitor. Was there another button? They'd ring again, then a third time, while Marlon studied them.

I walked back to the limo and smiled at Adrian to quash any idea that Marlon wasn't taking this meeting seriously or worse, had forgotten it. I said I was sure Marlon was around, he just hadn't heard the bell (which goes off like a klaxon everywhere). On my second return to the limo I realized

Adrian could be thinking I was an impostor, maybe Marlon Brando was in Brazil and had never heard of this scheme. Or of me.

Then Marlon drove up behind us. The gate opened and we all drove up to the house. Marlon made a couple of Kmart apologies for being late but appeared unruffled. We went inside and sat in the living room.

"So, Adrian," Marlon began, "you live in Hong Kong."

"My home is in Bali, it's my office that's in Hong Kong."

"God, I remember a beautiful experience I had in Bali. I walked up through these paddy fields, way up the side of the mountain, I guess it's actually a volcano, I must have gone three or four miles. I was alone, listening to the water tinkling down from one level to the next. Near the top I turned into the forest and came to this perfect little stream, so lively, so happy. I took off my clothes and sat in it naked, just let the water rush over me. I stayed there for hours."

"How long since you've been to Bali, Marlon?"

"Too long, must be twenty-five years."

"You should come back. We still have that lovely stream but also some new things. Twenty-five years ago we had only one or two very bad hotels, today we have some of the best in the world."

"One of them would be yours, correct?"

"Not quite. Two of them would be mine."

"Touché," Marlon said appreciatively. "The last time I was in Hong Kong I saw the most wonderful magazine, beautiful photography, extraordinary selection of subjects, it's called *Oriental Art and Architecture*. You know it, Adrian?"

"I do know it and I'm very glad to hear you like it."

"Do you subscribe to it?"

"I own it."

Adrian was impressive; when Marlon laid out his cards of esoterica, Adrian could match them, and often, in an offhand way, trump them. Marlon enjoyed Adrian's poise, his knowledge of many subjects.

At the end of the meeting Marlon said he wanted to move forward. Adrian could make all decisions as to structure, decor, everything. Marlon would offer his suggestions but final decisions would be Adrian's.

I had many meetings and phone and fax conversations with Adrian to construct the deal. Three months after Marlon and Adrian first met, it was closed. We gathered at Marlon's house for a last discussion that embraced everything—finances, environment, the Tahitian government, the opening of the hotel, when Marlon and I would visit Pukhet—within the next month, Marlon promised.

We shook hands all around, all pleased. I was particularly happy. Marlon had an excellent deal and an interesting new friend.

The next morning was bright and sunny and Marlon called early.

"The deal's off," he said.

Things like this had happened so many times with Marlon I didn't ask why.

"Okay," I said. As I was hanging up, he volunteered the reason.

"There's not enough money in it."

He had said it before during the three months; each time I'd gone through the deal with him again and each time he'd reconsidered and approved it. If you want greater income, I'd said, we can build a ten-story Holiday Inn. You don't want that. This is an excellent deal with the best partner for you.

Marlon's propensity for strangling good deals wouldn't matter all that much except that it's parts of his life that he squeezes to death. I think he still subscribes to the thought that some unsuspecting wealthy Japanese or Saudi will swing down the pike and he can lure him into his sideshow then fleece him.

From the very first Marlon said he wanted to have chapters in his book written by others. People who knew him but not all of whom liked him. Jack Beck, a TV documentary producer; Bob Hoskins, a boyhood friend; Rita Moreno; France Nuyen; his sisters Franny and Jocelyn; perhaps his children; and me. He said he'd pay each contributor a hundred thousand dollars.

I wasn't sure what he had in mind, but I didn't see the value in the concept that Marlon did.

"I think people want to read your story told by you," I said.

"They'll get my story, but I want to contrast my vision of myself with the way other people see me—my sisters, Rita, you, maybe my kids, that'll be interesting."

"It could be interesting, but it's a different book, I think. The value in your autobiography is what only you have lived, only you have seen."

"My life isn't something that belongs to me. The things I've experienced aren't my personal possessions. I want to show there's no such thing as truth, there are only perceptions—yours, mine, everybody's, all different."

"How many of these chapters do you see?"

"Maybe ten."

"Ten?"

"Ten opinions of me contrasted with my opinion of me will be fascinating."

"Ten people giving their versions of a specific event would be one thing, but ten writing whatever comes to their minds about you is broken matzo crackers."

Marlon remained unswayed. It occurred to me that he'd have substantially less to write if a good part of the book was authored by others.

When I pointed out that paying ten people $100,000 would cost him a million dollars, Marlon revised his idea of payments. He decided that if the chapter appeared in the book, the author would get $100,000. If it was not used, the author would get $50,000. As reality seeped in, he scaled the payments down step-by-step to a flat fee of $25,000. It was a groundless game since he wasn't negotiating with anyone.

Marlon was in hot pursuit of those assigned to write chapters; he had Alice hounding them, too. Eventually all of them came in. Except mine.

Marlon was distressed at what he read, even, in a few cases, unbelieving. He told me the writing was bad in general and that one of the chapters wasn't even about him, it was about the author's childhood, with an occasional reference to Marlon.

He asked again for my chapter. I was reluctant to do it, I didn't believe I or anyone else would be paid and of course we weren't, but that wasn't it. There was something odd. One evening Marlon said rather pointedly, "George, write everything, don't leave anything you want to say out . . . because that's what I'm going to do about you."

There's a Marlon statement. Write about me honestly and directly "because that's what I'm going to do about you." Does that mean he will retaliate if you write something he doesn't like. What awful thing might he say about you, why would he want to put so much about you in his autobiography?

But if you said, "Marlon, I'd rather not write a chapter," it would be equivalent to saying "I don't trust you." So here is a difficult moment with Marlon. He wants you to do what he's asked and there is no good reason to do it.

He said emphatically that all who wrote chapters would be paid. Those asked were close to him, family and friends, they trusted he was being truthful. To my knowledge none of them was paid anything.

For me the issue was friendship, at a certain point you set aside your reservations and do what your friend has asked. So I wrote my chapter. I should have qualified the terms of friendship for both of us before agreeing to do it.

In the chapter I touched on the question that still had not been answered, why he was writing his autobiography. I wrote:

After the long rigor to protect his privacy, forty years of successfully evading the press, why did Marlon want to write a tell-all autobiography? Long friendships had been ended because a friend spoke to a magazine about Marlon, one wrote a book about him, the highest possible crime. Why did he leave his seclusion now to join those he's loathed, who tell about themselves for money? Why does he invite others to write what they know of him?

I think it is because the purpose of the project is not to produce a book, it is to pull performers into a drama. Marlon's absorption is with how people behave and he will use all techniques to bring you under his microscope. He leads you with tales of his own lonely voyage out to the farthest rim of human existence, where it is sere and there are no tracks, where he survived without the unctions of everyday life, solitary by a frail fire. Yes, Marlon, I will try to be like you, as naked as you, as unafraid to reveal myself.

The autobiography must seem like a true enterprise, so Marlon worries at you to get your chapter done, wonders with you should he write in chronological order, should he use real names . . . and the hand that is ushering you into the arena moves unnoticed. You were talking about helping him write his book and it took you until now to realize that a game had begun, a game like all his, with lethal ramifications. You nearly forgot, though it's been taught you a hundred times, a relationship with Marlon is a killing field.

He rings the tocsin and secretaries, sisters, friends come to assist. As I have come. The territory he wants us to traverse is ambushed, under the rubric we're helping by writing about him, we will reveal ourselves. We all know inside that what we are writing is not an entry for Marlon's book, it is a way of giving ourselves to Marlon for his lab work. You know it but you do it anyway.

Marlon didn't discuss my chapter after he received it. Weeks later I asked what he thought. "There's nothing to talk about," he said. "Except, you think I kill deals. I don't kill deals." I was exasperated. I'd done what he asked, been honest, written him a chapter. Obviously he didn't like it, but that wasn't the deal, we should at least have discussed it. It never occurred to me to ask him for the twenty-five thousand dollars.

Others did. When Marlon didn't pay them or respond to their work, where was the twenty-five grand was a popular cry. Also, if the book was made into a film, would they be paid additionally? I had urged Marlon to have each contributor sign a contract that covered these aspects.

Marlon abandoned the idea of others writing chapters in his autobiography.

Random House hoped Marlon would work on the book even before the contract was finalized, and certainly begin writing as soon as possible once it was. He didn't. When two years went by and he had written only a few pages, he said his preoccupation with Christian and Cheyenne had prevented him from writing. Without question Marlon had lived through a devastating time, but his explanation for not writing was implausible.

It was during the Christian-Cheyenne drama that he decided to write the book; he was in the teeth of the gale then. On a number of occasions I asked, "Mar, are you sure you're going to write the book, sure you want to?" Each time the answer was definite, yes. He finally said, "George, you've got to stop asking, I am going to write the book, there is no possibility I won't write it."

He found time to film *Christopher Columbus* in Spain and before that to deliver long harangues about the script and rewrite part of it. In the two years since the contract signing, there had been time to work on his book.

Harry Evans showed patience. He and I conferred often about how to help Marlon accelerate, but Harry let the delivery dates go by. He reassured Marlon; he said that when Marlon was able to write, he was certain the extraordinary volume we all expected would be forthcoming.

Along the way, Harry and Joe Fox, Marlon's editor, suggested that Marlon work with me on the book. At one point Marlon called me and said, "I can't write this book, you do it. And it shouldn't be 'as told to,' it should be your book about me. Call it *Conversations with Marlon.*"

Finally, in February 1993, Harry Evans wrote Marlon that he reluctantly had to ask for the advance Marlon had received to be returned. He had now no reasonable hope the manuscript would be delivered in the foreseeable future. As an alternative, he suggested asking me to write a book about Marlon. He hoped Marlon would be able to afford me the time necessary to gather the information I would need.

Marlon thought about the suggestion for several days then called me.

"Harry's right, you should write the book with me, that's the way to get it done. It will be great for both of us, we can be anywhere in the world and have some laughs while we're working on it. I think you should get five percent all in for the job, that would be fair."

The prospect of us doing the book together was appealing, but I was surprised, though by this time I shouldn't have been, at the financial arrangement he proposed.

"Let's delay discussing my deal till I tell Harry the plan. I'm sure he'll be happy, as I am, Mar."

Harry was happy and wanted us to start immediately. On the matter of my fee, I decided to find outside advice. I asked Harry. He said the normal range for this kind of collaboration was twenty to thirty-three percent, though it could be as high as fifty. He thought twenty-five would be a fair price.

Sidney Sheldon is a good friend and I asked what he

thought. "Fifty percent," he said. "For that job, fifty percent, you may have to take less, but that's what you should get."

Mort Janklow asked what Marlon had proposed. When I told him five percent he said, "That's unbelievable, it's disgusting. It's worse, it's demeaning. Everybody knows what kind of friend you've been to Marlon, the way you handled his deal, that's the only word I can think of, demeaning."

I called Marlon. "Harry's got his tail up in the air. He thinks us collaborating is a wonderful plan, he wants us to start right away. I asked Harry what he thought I should get, Mar, he said the range was twenty to thirty-three percent. So maybe twenty-five percent would be fair."

"No, five percent."

"I don't want us to get into a negotiation, I'm not stuck on twenty-five percent, but that's a consensus figure from people in the industry."

"I don't give a shit what any of those assholes say, they have nothing to do with me. I'm me, I do things differently. Five percent is fair for you."

"Maybe neither one of us should use the word *fair*, Mar. Let me put it this way. If I got five percent, I would have made the deal for the book then coauthored it, all for ten percent. That's what an agent normally gets for simply making the deal."

"Okay, I'll have to find someone who'll do it for five percent."

We talked on a few minutes, nothing more of substance was said. Four days later Harry Evans called and told me Marlon had hired Robert Lindsey to write his autobiography with him.

"Did you know he was doing that, George?"

"No. We didn't agree on my fee, but I thought we'd discuss it again. No, I didn't know."

"Why didn't he talk with you again? Why couldn't you two work out a deal; it seems unthinkable. I have to accept Lindsey, he's an established writer, he's a good writer."

"He's a very good writer, I admire him. Anyway, I am Marlon's agent and his interests are my first responsibility. It's good Lindsey is aboard, the book should get finished now in a reasonable time. But, Harry, between you and me, don't be misled into thinking the problems are over. If form holds, Marlon and Lindsey will take off in a burst, then at some point Marlon will go cold, cold on Lindsey, cold on the book, and he'll be hard to find. You paid a lot of money and the book you publish mustn't be less than the one we talked about. That would be a disservice to Marlon and you."

"I know what you mean. We'll get it done."

Two days later Marlon called. "I've got to decide what direction to go in with the Tahiti rainwater, need to know if you want to do it."

His ploys don't have the old speed, they're transparent now—see if George is angry by bringing up the rainwater deal. He's already turned it down, but I, Marlon, will act as if I've forgotten.

"I think we have some other business to talk about first, Mar. Harry told me you've hired another writer."

"Yup, Robert Lindsey. You didn't want to do it, so I got him."

"I didn't say I didn't want to do it, it was just the opposite, we both said what a great time we'd have, we could be writing it anywhere. The problem wasn't if I wanted to do it, the issue was money."

"Not accepting five percent was tantamount to saying you didn't want to do it."

"Who made that rule? After all that's gone on with this book—with our whole lives—you, not Harry, should have told me you were hiring somebody else. That's a courtesy I would have given to a stranger."

"What about the rainwater?"

"I should have heard it from you, Mar. There are obligations that go with being friends. It's understandable if they can't make a deal, but they have to end as friends."

"What do you want to do about the rainwater?"

"I'll think about it."

"I hear more no than yes in that."

"Probably."

"How much time do you need, a week?"

"A day."

"I can call you this time tomorrow?"

"Yeah."

"Okay, I'll call you tomorrow."

I sent him a fax saying I had no taste for doing anything with him now including the rainwater. I felt no emotion, only that it was twilight for Marlon and me. No path was in view that could bring us together again. He had broken the sacred loop, he'd seized this five percent like a witch doctor's rattle and refused to consider its appropriateness or fairness.

I thought of Marlon and Sugar Ray Robinson. In the 1950s Sugar Ray was the middleweight champion of the world. He was supreme in this century, maybe in the history

of boxing. He had murder in both hands and he was quick—
Lord, he was fast, slip your punch and be inside battering
your body then outside taming you with his left before you
saw him again.

In the glory days of the fifties you could liken Sugar Ray to
Marlon or Marlon to Sugar Ray. Golden boys both. And
Sugar Ray could fight dirty, he was the best at that, too.
Thumb in your eye, rake you with the laces, crack you with
the elbow, bite on the break or frighten you with his talk in
the clinches.

The years went by and that old thief time cut away at Sugar
Ray's speed and power. The champ could still fight dirty,
though, so he'd win some. But at the end, when the grace and
the class were gone and Sugar Ray was overage and shouldn't
have been in the ring anymore, all that was left to him was the
ability to fight dirty.

You could liken Marlon to Sugar Ray. That's how I felt then.

Neither Marlon nor I knew it, but we were at the beginning
of a seven-year period—from 1993 to 2000—when we didn't
talk at all. That proved to be a towering loss to me because I
was about to pass through a time of sadness and difficulty.

14

February 18, 1994

Max, my eleven-year-old son, as dear to me as anything in this world has ever been, died today.

The day Max was born, Marlon came to the hospital to see him and congratulate his mother. After the visit Marlon and I went to an Italian restaurant in Santa Monica where they sang operatic arias. Marlon always keeps that cordon sanitaire around him, guarding against being used by those with whom he's in public, but this was one of our most relaxed times, I had a new son, we were happy.

Marlon was an integral part of that time. He'd taken a long look at my new wife, Bonnie, when I showed up with this twenty-five-year old from the South. He studied her from a distance then up close and pronounced her sound of tooth and hoof. He gave us a spa for our new house as a wedding present, he was at the stag dinner Cliff Perlman gave for me. He was at our wedding. One night he and his Japanese girlfriend

sneaked into our house while we were out for dinner and were lying on our bed eating ice cream when we came home.

A few days after Max's birth, Bonnie and Max were home from the hospital and the happy time continued. At the doctor's office the day Max was six and a half months old, the doctor surveyed him confidently. "He'll be crawling any day now," the doctor said, knowledgeable, smiling. We smiled, too, and our conversation that night glowed with plans for Max's future.

But Max didn't crawl. A week went by and we said, "Well, he's a late bloomer, some kids just take longer, they want to think it over before they get into this world." We exchanged other platitudes to rationalize the tardiness.

But I knew Max should be crawling. His serenity, his beauty were in bloom, but his movements had settled down and were quiet. I stole into the den one night and sat down by the big dictionary and first looked up *multiple sclerosis*. It wasn't that; the symptoms for that illness had nothing to do with crawling. I sat back thinking about where else, what else, and the words *muscular dystrophy* came to me. Could that have anything to do with Max? I found the entry and the clinical, merciless words flew at my eyes: "Any of a group of hereditary diseases characterized by progressive wasting of muscles."

I read on. Max fit the description of a child with one of the serious dystrophies, one of the lethal ones. My heart jumped. I left the dictionary, went over and looked out the window, then came back and read it again. Wrapped in cold octopus tentacles, I closed the book and went to our bedroom and didn't say anything to Bonnie.

I told only the doctor what I'd found. On seeing Max again, he recommended we have a muscle biopsy done. We agreed, a female surgeon did the operation, the tissue went to the lab.

Three days later the doctor called and said he wanted to come to the house that night and discuss the results.

In this part of the century a doctor volunteering a house call at night could only mean desperately bad news.

The doctor brought a pad and a soft pencil and he sat on the sofa opposite Bonnie and me. He drew a diagram of nerves coming out of the spinal column.

"Spinal muscular atrophy," he said, "or Werdnig-Hoffman's disease, as it is also called, means the neurons from the spinal cord don't charge the muscles. The muscles will not develop and the victim will have only the most limited muscular capacities. If both parents have the same recessive gene—and which gene that is no one knows—the child will have a one-in-four chance of being born with this illness."

Beautiful, unknowing Max had been pulled out of the line of healthy babies and forced into that cold lottery.

"Bronchial or pulmonary infections are especially danger-ous," the doctor went on, "because the weak diaphragm mus-cles can't produce enough of a cough. When the symptoms present early, as they have with Max, life expectancy is brief."

Her senses spinning and not completely grasping what she'd heard, Bonnie said, "Then . . . what is the prognosis?"

Perhaps the doctor was unsteady himself, but his response was staccato and harsh. "There is no prognosis, he's going to die."

I cannot write successfully about that moment. You have to be the parent and have those words stabbed into your heart. To you, of all the parents in the world, they have been spo-ken, words that cannot be rescinded or recalled.

Bonnie seemed to fall inward, tears flooded from her eyes. I put my arm around her. It was awkward. Looking on was this man we hardly knew, this messenger who carried the news that brought an earthquake to our lives.

"I think we understand," I said. My voice sounded metallic, as if it were being played through a filter. "It's probably better we be alone now."

"Yes, of course," the doctor said, and stood up. "I'm sorry to have brought such sad news. I'm at your disposal if there's anything you want to talk about."

"Thanks," I said. I walked him to the door and came back and sat beside Bonnie. I held her and thought of Max sleeping in his little bed upstairs. We sat motionless, we had lost our foothold on earth. We decided to get in the car and drive. We drove silently, our minds turning the information over and over.

I thought how awful it was that Marlon and I weren't in touch. If he were aware of my painful passage, he'd have been here in a second. And stayed.

Bonnie broke the silence in the car. "We'd better start planning the funeral."

"Jesus, not yet, we don't know how long he's going to live, maybe there's something we can do, maybe there's research going on somewhere, we have to see, we have to think about—" In the middle, tears leaped out of me and a baying sound. I couldn't see the road; I pulled over and stopped, awash. Then Bonnie cried, too. Helplessly we sat in the front seat of the car bobbing and sobbing toward the windshield.

When Max didn't die right away, I began to think about which was worse, losing him quickly or getting to know him, to love him, and in his teens at the latest, to participate in his death. Marlon came to Max's first birthday party. He was real, present. He talked of how Max had reshaped me, he described the changes he saw in me. Of all the long hours Marlon and I spent on the telephone before we stopped talking, there could only have been a few that didn't have tales of Max in them. Not long after we learned of Max's condition Marlon said, "You've got your work cut out, Georgie, that little boy embodies all your nightmares, no control, unable to move, to defend yourself, at the mercy of others."

Because of Max we moved out of Los Angeles and built a home in Palm Springs. Each day began with thoughts of Max, what he needed, where he had to go, how he had to be dressed. They ended with a request for a story or a bite of chocolate, some means to prolong the day. Then the calmness of a tired little boy drifting off, and the vigil of Bonnie and Lupe, Max's nanny, and me began.

We slept until Max awoke and needed to be turned onto his other side or on his back. That was a privilege granted in this life, to be Max's guarantee you would be there to help him.

Max succumbed, too swiftly, before we could prepare, but as the doctors had prophesied, to a pulmonary infection that swept through his body.

I've thought it would have been good for Marlon to be here in this time after Max's death. The light from Max's life might have lightened the landscape he was living in with his own children.

I wondered what Marlon did think when he heard that Max died. It would be difficult for him to write me, but I think he'd want to say something. Truly it is odd to be making this passage from one theater of life to another without talking with Marlon. He would come closest to understanding, no meretricious sadness, no gratuitous mourning, a man friend who'd say, "Sit down a second, Georgie, let it come."

Federal Express is a good organization, they called this morning to say they had a letter for me but the wrong address. The package they were trying to deliver was addressed to where we lived seven years ago when we were building our house. The regular driver was off—I told them where I lived.

The letter was from Marlon. About Max. Marlon must have decided that whatever else was going on, Max's death must be spoken about. The note is meant to comfort Bonnie and me and it does that. It also brings a new sadness. I keep it on my desk a long time and think about Marlon and Max and the bewildering traversal that is life. I hesitate to quote from the note, doing so raises the flag of betrayal, but one part might be heard: "Max is one of the few people I ever knew that merited a salute—I salute him now. Let us take delight in welcoming him to the freedom he longed for. His new day has begun. Good morning, Max."

Good morning, Max. Only Marlon would think of that to say.

I wrote Marlon a brief note.

Dear Mar,

Thanks for the letter. Your thoughts on Max's death were beautifully expressed.

Strange to pass through this hour and not have a conversation with you about it.

Best to leave it all lie. How you and I got here or even where we are—we were right when we said it all doesn't mat-

ter. It doesn't matter if we knew each other a long time. It doesn't matter if we harmed it, it wouldn't matter if we healed it. You're good to have written.

It was not very long after Max's death that Franny, Marlon's sister, died. I wrote to him.

Dear Mar,

It is my turn to send a thought to you about a loss through death. What words to use? I can't say the sampler aphorisms I have recently come to know so well, she's happier now, she's released from her pain.

Fuck death, you used to say. And now? Now that Franny is gone, fuck death still? What is death now, a friend, a menace, a meaninglessness? You and I need no more reminders of our mortality. But we'll get them anyway, my sister Patsy or Jocelyn or you or I or Cloris will drop. We are those Moiseyev dancers that flow around the stage as if on rollers then disappear into the wings.

Still, it is a sunshiny day down here. We have an abundant and gorgeous crop of roses. I hope you are seeing some sunshine and roses, Mar. Looking at you above the tangle of what separates us I send you—what—what is allowed to send? We need a rule book to tell us what is allowed and not allowed. I send you my feelings, they are not confined by rules and toward you they are as they always will be, rich and many. And loving.

A dear friend of mine, Mike Hill, is probably the best researcher in the country. Among the prominent literary figures for whom he does research is Pulitzer Prize winner David McCullough; in fact, it was through David that I met Mike.

One day while I was talking with Mike, he asked how things were going between Marlon and me. I said we still hadn't talked after nearly seven years.

"You two remind me of Thomas Jefferson and John Adams," he said.

"That's pretty good company, Mike. Where's the similarity?"

Mike told me the story. Adams and Jefferson had been great friends through the revolution and the years after it, then they had political differences and didn't speak for eleven years. Finally Adams wrote Jefferson and in the letter he said, "You and I ought not to die before we have explained ourselves to each other."

When the two were reunited again, their correspondence was "rich and voluminous, they talked on every subject, their health, religion, philosophy and reflected on the past and on the future," wrote Lester Cappon, editor of the Adams-Jefferson letters.

That story took residence in me. I thought of what Adams and Jefferson had missed in not being in touch during that long separation. I thought about Marlon and me. After seven years the reasons we were apart seemed less important than the need that we come together again. Actually we had both begun to search for a bridge, we were both asking about each other through people who knew us.

Then one day, four years ago now, I picked up the phone and called Marlon. It was pathetically simple, no looking back, no painful review, we were happy to hear each other's voice again, and we started talking like the Marlon and George we'd always been.

"So many subjects crowd upon me that I know not with

which to begin," wrote Adams. It could have been Marlon or me saying it. Adams also said that he felt friendship was "one of the crowning glories of mankind."

Marlon's and my disquisitions may not rival those of Adams and Jefferson, but we are back in stride now, this afternoon we explored the subject of laughter. When you think about it, we said, it's a bizarre response to something we've called "funny." Our phrenic nerve jumps, we cackle, bare our teeth, bob, touch one another, our tear glands activate. We say whatever the phenomenon of laughter is, we couldn't have gotten this far in life without it, it's the most precious thing we share.

We were aglow at being back together. But more drama awaited, our ability to create it had not waned.

There is a cream-colored, short-sleeved shirt hanging in my closet, it has a button-down collar and a polo insignia on the breast. There are five wide bloodstains on the shirt. They were bright red the day the blood was deposited there, but with age they have darkened to the color of dark mud. The night I took the shirt off I hung it in the closet and every time I enter I see it again, as I had planned. The shirt has something to do with dogs and Marlon and me.

A year ago my third son with Cloris, George Jr., now in his forties, came to stay with my son Graves and me. He brought with him a tiny dog, a black Pomeranian, that had once belonged to his daughter, my granddaughter, Skye. But now Skye had another dog and this one had come back to George. He brought two small dog-carrying cases. He said the dog was completely at home in these cylindrical canvas bags with the mesh at either end, so she went with him to restaurants and other public places and nobody knew she was there.

I didn't cotton to this Pomeranian because I had never had a little dog; pets of that size didn't seem, well, manly. What made this creature even less appealing to me was the name Skye had given her, Baby Bear. It might have been an appropriate moniker for a young girl's dog, but it was a discord in this house with three large men. But the dog knew nothing of my reservations about her; she was content with her heritage from the nobility of Pomerania and she walked the house in her proud, sprightly way.

The Lord, as we know, works in mysterious ways His wonders to perform, and at about this time He became active in rearranging our lives. When George returned to Los Angeles, he moved into a building that didn't allow dogs. So, as Graves and I waved good-bye to George, there was a third entity on the ground between us also wishing him Godspeed. The dog stayed behind.

On one of the first mornings after George left, I put the dog on a leash and took her to a nearby country mall that had an outdoor restaurant I frequented. As we approached the eating area, an elderly woman saw us and exclaimed to her friends, "Oh, look at that big man with that tiny dog!" The others craned to see. It was humiliating because it confirmed my inner knowledge that I looked ridiculous with this cameo canine.

As I passed the table, the woman, charmed by the dog's size and self-confidence, leaned down to pet her. She looked up to me and said, "What's her name?"

It would not be possible to mouth the words *Baby Bear,* so I mumbled, "She, um, she doesn't have a name."

"She doesn't have a name?!" The woman's face bloomed with both incredulity and accusation. She turned to her fellow diners for confirmation that this was a lunatic statement. She turned back to me with a look that said my last remark was unacceptable, I should give it another go.

"Well," I said, "she did have a name at one time, but it went away." I pulled on the leash and dog and I marched on, they could gnaw on that bone for a while.

Graves was sixteen years old and six-four, and he and the dog were even more out of symmetry than the dog and I. We agreed she had to have a different name, something at the opposite end of the spectrum from the sugary Baby Bear. We decided to call her Butch.

She adapted quickly, with admirable grace, and in the days that followed, this tiny creature, once derided, once scorned for her lack of height and depth of chest, not only became admissible in our home, she became essential to its life. She was the other presence that knew my patterns of movement, of eating, of preparing to leave. When I rose from my desk chair, she would look over from her perch on the sofa to see which of the known avenues I was about to walk. Then she fell in with me. At night, when I went to bed, she bounced up and went directly to a neutral corner at the bottom. She knew I didn't like her to lean against my leg because as tiny as she was, her body emitted astonishing heat and exerted real pressure.

She would lie at that far corner then later move to a pillow opposite me but not so close that she intruded on my sleeping sphere.

As she came to know me, I came to know her. I had grown accustomed not only to her face but to her gaiety, her walk with the light prance of an Arabian stallion, petite and proud and perfect.

Since Graves was at school all day, Butch and I spent long hours together. We were explorers of the neighborhood, Huck and Tom rafting down the Mississippi. We shared moods; if I was melancholy she knew and would sigh with me. If I was laughing or expressing positive emotions, her body language said, "Good, I'm with you, pal."

When Graves and I drove, Butch would put her back feet on the front edge of the backseat and her forelegs on the console of the front seat, which placed her head between us. The three of us would look down the road of life, ready for the first marauder who crossed our path. She enjoyed her equality of station and exercised her rights. If she wanted a more prominent position, she would paw at my right arm, a signal that I should raise it so she could move into my lap. "It will be better this way," her look said as she curled into her new position.

So, where once we were two, now we were three. Three hearts sworn to protect the household, three souls bound by the oath of d'Artagnan and his Musketeers, all for one and one for all.

Because of the seven-year gap in my friendship with Marlon, Graves had heard me talk about Marlon but he had never met him. He wanted to, and Marlon wanted to meet Graves, so on a Saturday, we drove up to Marlon's house.

We passed through the gate, traveled the three hundred yards, then took the left fork up the hill. I stopped in the parking area just below the house, opened the windows a few inches for Butch, then Graves and I left the car and went into the house. Angela was there to greet us. Then Marlon came along the hall from his bedroom in his traditional garb, kimono with obi, fleece-lined bedroom slippers. He stopped and surveyed Graves for a long moment. This sustained appraisal could have been uncomfortable, but for Graves it wasn't; he smiled as Marlon assessed him in detail. Then Marlon came over and stood next to Graves and looked up at him.

"You ought to get nosebleeds living up there," he said. Then he gave Graves a hug and Graves put his arms around Marlon. Family.

Graves said he wanted to get a bowl of water for Butch.

"Bring her in," Marlon said.

"No," I said, "she's happy in the car and she's never been around dogs that size."

"They wouldn't do anything to her," Marlon said. "They'll be fine with her."

"No, she's all right in the car." I waved to Graves to get the water and bring it to her.

It was a relaxed and happy afternoon. Graves and Marlon got on beautifully from the start. That they shared the same sense of humor surprised Marlon at first then he realized Graves's humor had its origins in mine. His immediate and growing affection for Graves was plain; he'd had such unhappiness with Christian and Cheyenne that I think he was lonely for something, somebody filial.

We got into the pool, which is almost Olympic size and was heated to ninety-two degrees. Marlon was, as customarily, enormous, and he brought out his weights and showed us the exercises he does with them in the water. We all had a go at it. Graves is a leader on his school's swimming and water-polo teams, Marlon was impressed with his dolphin moves.

When we got out I went to check on Butch, making certain first the dogs were inside the gate.

"Bring her out, George," Marlon said.

"No, she's fine there." I just didn't want to have any kind of a situation with her and the big dogs.

"They're not going to hurt her, that's the last thing they'd do."

"No, she loves being in the car."

I let Butch out for a leak, put her back, saw that she was okay, and went back to the house. The pleasant mood continued. Marlon's affection for Graves was a balm to me. He was curious about everything: Graves's classes, his grades, his teachers, his coaches. Graves was gentlemanly and humorous in response.

It was getting dark and Marlon asked what we wanted for dinner. There was a good Italian restaurant that would send up whatever we wanted. We made our choices and Angela took them down. About a half hour later it was time to check on Butch again.

"George, bring her out, she'll be fine," Marlon said.

"No, Mar, I'll just feel better if she stays there. She's just a twig and I don't want anything to happen."

"Nothing's going to happen. Christ, I know these dogs, I live with them, they're harmless with another animal, especially a small one. Bring her in."

"Really, Mar, she's okay where she is."

"You're crazy, let her share the grounds, get her out of the car."

"Okay." I said it even though I was aware that I was acquiescing to Marlon's persistence rather than obeying my own good reasoning.

Graves went out the front door into the garden and over to the car. Marlon and I stayed in the living room. Graves brought Butch back and set her down outside the front door. The rottweiler and the mastiff went right for her. A scream came out of Graves as they chased her down, their barks coming like thunder, Graves's yells on top of them.

I ran out thinking I could get there before anything bad happened because Butch was so quick, she'd be able to outrun them.

I was wrong, they had terrified her. She had lain down as they came at her, rolled over on her back as if to say, "Please don't hurt me." One of them slashed her belly open and her intestines came bursting out. Small, curved tubes, all that were needed for a dog that size.

I held her in my arms as her terrified eyes lost focus and became preoccupied with oncoming death. Her little purple tongue fluttered and with her last searching breaths she pumped her blood onto my shirt. This angel, this gift of light and gladness, this matchless little girl, had been killed.

Graves and I put her in a towel and laid her in the trunk of the car. Back inside Marlon's house it was unearthly. Somewhere inside me was a maniacal scream: "Marlon, why did you insist that I bring her in, you didn't know what you were talking about." And there was a scream at myself. "Why did you listen to him, you know better than anyone he wants to get you to go along with him no matter what it is he's saying. You had to be insane."

We talked in fragments, Marlon, Angela, Graves, and I. Graves and I couldn't eat, he was destroyed, both of us felt guilty, hysterical, lost.

"Don't blame yourself, Mar," I said. "That's nature, animals do what the instincts tell them to do."

Marlon got a look on his face like nothing I have ever seen. It was a Balinese fright mask. I guess it was meant to show grief, but it was beyond looking human. His whole system of glands and organs was maxed out, his face was red orange and distorted as if he were in the last throe of giving birth or trying to take the most massive shit of his life. The only explanation I could think of was that this expression of grief/torture/disbelief would say that no one in such pain could be blamed for Butch's death.

Graves and I dug a hole up on the mountainside near our house and laid Butch in it.

It was to have been a happy visit to Marlon's; instead, Graves and I were bathed in the mysteries of this planet, the randomness of the life upon it, and the sadness, beyond sadness, we are sometimes forced to bear.

Butch's radiant soul has not left me. Still today, when I rise from my desk chair, subconsciously I expect to see her lift her head, then I will hear her feet hit the parquet floor, and I will find the look in her eyes that asks, "Where we going, George?"

Maybe that's not what her eyes are asking, maybe the query is, "Did you have to go along with Marlon's insistence that you take me out of the car?"

15

I am still in that long recent night in Marlon's guesthouse, lying on my side, and the trolls of the past circle around me. I find the past to be a disorderly place. Faces that were part of one chapter of life float unattached to era or event. Emotions blink in the semidarkness, memories lie with their legs over one another.

During the Third Reich, Nazi doctors determined that the human psyche is most defenseless against shock and fear between the hours of 3:30 and 4 A.M. So when the SS pulled Jews out of their homes, they stormed through the doors at exactly 3:45 to produce maximum fright and disarray.

I am in that hour now and what Homer called "the rosy-fingered dawn" seems a galaxy away. A question comes cometlike: What will be the future? It is not a gentle, philosophical inquiry, the words burn, cold, menacing, vivid. The question intensifies the feeling of vulnerability because old age is coming.

Mentally I stand on my hind legs, forepaws raised against the oncoming dragon, but old age does not line up in uniformed battalions, it comes shadowy, silent, from all compass points.

In that time just ahead is the certainty that death is nigh and you are nearing its depot. While you approach, death reveals nothing of itself; like an image of the Buddha with half-shut eyes, it waits. There is no Siegfried line, no seawall to keep it away, there is submission to the thin, mottled skin that covers the backs of your hands.

Once, on a rum-soaked night on Tetiaroa, Marlon and I jeered at old age. We lampooned the drove of elders carrying their folding chairs to the seaside area reserved for them in Miami Beach, the ancients applauded for playing dorky tennis, praised for electing to have cosmetic surgery, admired in cruise commercials for hints of twilight sexuality. How is it, we wanted to know, that old men in America all know to wear baseball caps and plaid polyester jackets that consistently don't match the plaid in the polyester pants they're wearing? We mandated that suicide bombers be recruited to blow up Buick sedans that sported a "Foxy Grandma" bumper sticker. The image of the purple-haired senior in the passenger seat taking on the entire bowling team was too hideous. Nothing could ever make us be part of that pageant of asthmatic wheezes, failing sight, corroding memory, arthritic digits, those afflictions came to others, not us.

Now I see, in old age you are compelled, compelled to feel the way you don't want to feel, to walk the way you don't want to walk, to stoop and step timidly, to yield control of the senses, of the spine, of the bowels and bladder. With these losses comes a greater one, the vanishing of dignity. You perform the old person's pavane while death claws into the viscera, flattens the lungs, inflates the prostate, shrinks the liver. No respect, no recalling that this organism once looked into the mirror to see if it was well dressed and would be attractive at work.

I have resisted sleep through most of this long night in the winter of 2004 in Marlon's guest room. Now, in the stillness of morning, thoughts come of how complex my friendship with Marlon has been over the course of forty-eight years. We have ambushed each other and administered major pain. And often exquisite care. I've put on an Aunt Jemima bandanna and swept up the mess of Marlon's life; to my dark hour he has brought patience and steadfastness and led me to the morning he promised would come. He has called me in the deep of night when depression assailed him, horrors burgeoning out of his imagination, shrikes and dybbuks that boost his heartbeat to a dismaying cadence. As we talk, despair and doom settle on him. He'll take a Valium, I agree he should. Sometimes no pharmaceutical aid, let come what will. He is brave in those times, the bouts with the hellhounds inside call for the greatest courage.

One image of Marlon I turn to often. He is standing on the edge of his island on Tetiaroa ankle-deep in the water. A large frigate bird is downwind starting a run at the fish Marlon is holding out. Huge wings, heavy body, the thing is coming with a rush, it could take Marlon's hand off at the wrist. Eyes bulging, neck extended, inches from Marlon's body, whomp, it snags the fish and the wings pump skyward. Marlon shades his eyes and watches the flight, the fish bobbing in the bird's beak. He's fastened on the sight, seeing every detail. In his mind he is soaring with the frigate bird.

Marlon will die by the sea. Wherever he dies he'll go for his whitening to the sea. There will be a funeral cortege, people and things from his life—his dogs, a trail of hermit crabs, a table he made, cutouts of the women he said "I love you" to, electric eels. I'll be there.

We'll string along the beach silhouetted against the Pacific, turning, dipping, wheeling, we'll have music, a bagpiper, for no sound so well carries the lament of death, the mystery of departure. And Tahitian drums, they seduced Marlon. In his fit days he'd dance the tamure at night on the beach, snap his hips right, left, up, down, a ferocious sexuality. We'll slap him on the head to remind him of how he was then.

He would want me to be funny and I will, I'll imitate him receiving the award at the General Assembly of the UN. He had brand-new shoes on, and as he went up the steps, the soles slipped on the carpet and flashed their blond newness back at us. And the magnificent movie star was a little boy going to his first dance class. He loved to hear me tell that one.

I will lie down beside him, a last closeness. Sad and mourning I'll be in spite of the hours we spent belittling death. Then I'll go out alone with him in a pirogue, we'll float over the coral heads, so luminous, so lovely. I'll dump him into the water and the skinny canoe will tip dangerously, then it will tip the other way, and I'll go in the sea with him. At the end, comedy for us.

But Marlon will have weights on like Edmond Dantes escaping from the Château d'If, and I will not. He'll sink and I will dog-paddle and watch. And little Buddy Brando, born to Dorothy Pennebaker and Marlon Brando, but left alone by them, will have finished his breathing time on earth. And left me a world turned dark without him.

It won't happen like that. The family, however that word is refashioned to encompass the collection of people who bear his name, will do what they think ought to be done. The movie industry will claim him, there will be testimonials, retrospectives, significant analyses. All that. And maybe I'll die first.

Yes, how would that be? Marlon would pull up under the pier where I lie, stand in his dory, and knock on the planks.

"Georgie?"

He won't hear anything, so he'll knock again. I've always been there when he wanted to talk.

"Georgie?"

"I'm dead, Mar, so save the knocking."

"Where are you?"

"Out on a space current sixty thousand feet high. Death isn't a traversal into another plane of existence, Mar, it's a dousing, a lightning bug going out. All that's left of me is the pieces in your mind, my head, my shoulder, the way I walked, my smile, they merge for a moment, but you can't remember me whole. In all the reeling vertigo that was life, Mar, there were only a couple of great ideas. You and me as friends was a grand one. It's over and gone, but it had a Dixieland beat and didn't we ramble. *Adios, muchacho.*"

This I wrote down five months ago on that restless night in Marlon's guest room.

Sunday, June 27, 2004

The color of his voice, the stress, the chord of pain shattered the Sunday afternoon. On the computer display in front of me was a page from the book I was writing about Marlon and me. It had taken me deep into our past, and when the phone rang I almost didn't pick it up, not wanting to be distracted. It was Marlon.

Long ago he and I had dispensed with telephone salutations. It came from, once again, his distaste for the ordinary, he disliked the grunts that begin most phone conversations— What's up? How ya doing? So this afternoon, as always, he just began. That part was ordinary; everything else—the emotion in his voice, that he seemed to be talking from a distant island where he'd been stripped of everything familiar—was not ordinary.

"I can't take it anymore, Georgie, I don't care, I have to hear your voice," were his first words.

Most of the time his calls began with a leisurely recitation of what was on his mind. He'd poke along in a donkey cart, pause to examine a side thought or explore a feeling, and I was invited to argue with or add to the discourse. Not today, today Marlon was being forced to travel faster through his emotions than he was able to.

"I love you, Georgie, those years we had, we own them, they're ours, forty-eight years. I'm starting to cry. I don't care, I just wanted to talk for a minute . . . I'd take a bullet for you, Georgie."

"Oh, Mar . . ." It wasn't a statement, it was a fearful response.

"It's okay, it doesn't matter, we don't have to do anything.

I just wanted to tell you if you had a cunt we'd have been married a long time ago." We laughed. "I'm crying, Georgie, I can't help it."

"Jesus, Mar, we have to see each other, I'll come up, I'll come up Wednesday, I'll be there Wednesday."

"You don't have to, it's okay."

"No, I'm coming, Mar, I'll see you Wednesday."

The old Marlon wasn't there. The rogue lover, master manipulator, sly, tempting, clever, compelling, talented Marlon, it was not he on the telephone. Speaking was an organism in the process of being ravaged, the body sped through by a ninja force that darted north, south, forayed into his organs, plugged his breathing. Unconditional surrender had been demanded, but nature did not seem to have waited for his acquiescence; it continued its hellish rip through his body.

On Tuesday, Angela called to ask if I knew what time I'd be arriving the next day.

"I plan to be there around two," I said.

"That's fine, that'll be perfect, see you then."

I understood the reason for the call, the hour didn't matter, Marlon wasn't going anywhere, he'd asked her to make sure I was coming.

Vee, Angela's sister, accompanied me down the teak flooring of the corridor. I entered Marlon's room. The bed was on my right, Angela was either kneeling on the floor or sitting on a low stool at its foot. I walked around her, Marlon was lying on his right side. There was a gray-white stubble on his face, probably a two-week growth. His eyes were at the end of dark hollow chambers, his cheeks concave. The oxygen connections were in his nostrils and his face showed he was in pain. He had on a cotton robe that was pulled open, his backside was exposed. It was on that area that Angela was working.

Angela gave me a smile of hello, Marlon's attention was on what she was doing. His look to me was not one of greeting, rather a glance to someone who was sharing the activity. There was a swivel desk chair just to the left of Angela, I sat into it and became part of the goings-on. She was cleaning his rectal area; it was taking some doing and some time. No embarrassment was felt by any of us. That was our way, it was not necessary to pause and say hello.

After a while Marlon looked over at me. "Every time I cough, something gets released inside and it comes out."

Then I understood. Angela was cleansing the area and rolling the residue into a Kleenex ball which she then put into the wastebasket.

"Are you an RN, Angela?" I asked.

"No," she said. "I wanted to be but my father said no, he wanted me to study accounting, so that's what I did. My sister Vee is a nurse."

Angela had had to do this cleaning operation many times and the area was raw. She hit a particularly painful spot and Marlon reacted visibly. He rolled his eyes and pursed his lips and made his discomfort funny. I laughed.

"It's good to see you're still acting, Mar."

"That's not acting, this is the face of real pain."

"No question the pain is real and you registered that. But with those burlesque eyes, you also gave a report on how brutal the pain was, which made Angela and me laugh."

"I'm going to do to her what she's doing to me so she'll know how it feels," he said. Angela and I laughed. "She uses an alligator brush to scrape with the plates turned the wrong way." Marlon was nervously watching her work.

Angela and I flicked a smile to each other, it was clear that Marlon's pain was not just from that raw area, it came from the assaults inside as well.

I sat silently while Angela finished up. She rose; she still had on the white plastic medical gloves.

"Would you like some lunch?" she asked me.

"Angela, after watching what your hands have been doing, the idea of them fixing me lunch . . ." She laughed, Marlon smiled. "I'm not hungry right now, thanks."

The black desk chair I was sitting in was not in Marlon's line of sight. I got up and started to move it.

"Mar, I think it will be easier if I'm more in front of you." I started to pull the chair over to face it toward him, but there was too much furniture in the way. Angela and I pushed a large table back, then I positioned the chair where Marlon and I would be looking at each other. Evidently no one had been here talking with Marlon in some time.

"Marlon, I'm going to do some errands," Angela said.

"How long will it take?"

"Oh, the bank in the valley, an hour and a half maybe."

"Okay, keep in touch."

Angela left the room.

"What a piece of luck to have found her, Mar," I said.

"She's sent from heaven."

"Does everything, started as the maid, became your assistant, now she runs the whole estancia—and with equal aplomb repairs your ailing ass."

"She's a giant."

Marlon's focus was split between our conversation and the painful disturbances in his body.

"How are you spending your days, Georgie, what are you thinking about?" he said.

"Taking a new look at the old questions, Mar. I'm reading a biography of Descartes. He had these turgid dreams several nights in a row and on the last night he saw, written in Latin, the words *Quod vitae spectabor iter*. What path shall I follow in life? It's a little adolescent, but that's the question for me today as much as it was when I was twenty."

I talked slowly, articulating each word. The story wasn't important, I just wanted an echo of the way we bring interesting subjects to each other. Marlon was looking at me with the half-open mouth and hollow stare that said he was somewhere else as well as here.

"Descartes was raised a Catholic," I continued, "and early in his life he started to question the dogma of the Church. That curiosity, not accepting the common picture of reality, led him to invent a system he called solipsism . . ."

Marlon's eyes had closed, I stopped talking. After a few moments his eyes opened again. "Go on," he said softly.

We were along the road of, in the business of, dying. It was methodical, turn out the lights one by one, close the doors.

"Solipsism was a method of systematic doubt. Descartes sat alone in a little hut in the French Alps and first doubted the existence of everything outside the hut, then everything inside, then the chair he sat on, and ultimately himself. He came at the end to what is now a famous statement in philosophy: *Cogito ergo sum*—I think, therefore I am."

Marlon nodded. "That's good, Georgie."

He had a pillow between his knees. On the bed, above and

to the left of his head, was a Kleenex box; to the left of that was the phone; he could easily touch either, he only had to reach across and up with his left hand.

In the minutes since Angela had left, the issue from his anus had increased; now he reached up, took a tissue, and in an arcing motion delivered it to the painful area. He repeated the process with regularity as we talked. After placing three or four of the tissues, he gathered them together with his left hand, inspected what was in them, then rolled the mass into a ball and flung it to the wastebasket. Raising his head to look was too arduous, so most of the time he missed; the area alongside the bed was covered with used tissues.

"It's balletic, Mar, the way you float those tissues from the box down to your butt."

"I never had the right credentials before, but now I can say it with full authority, I've got a pain in the ass," he said.

I smiled. His eyes closed in a soft, accepting way. He seemed to be asleep or in an area close to it. His eyelids moved then lifted halfway.

"How long?" Marlon said, his eyes closed again then partly opened. "How long since reproductive fluid from your testicles went past your urethra and out through your dick?"

Here was the very bedrock of us. With death in the room, this question would come to him. His eyes closed again, I waited for them to open.

"It's been a while, Mar, three or four hours anyway."

The movement of his lips suggested a smile. We sat calmly, easy-listening music had been playing through the speakers across the room. Marlon opened his eyes.

"That's my favorite song," he said. " 'What'll I Do?' "

"Do you know who wrote it?" I asked.

"Yeah, but I can't think of it, who?"

"You know what ASCAP is, Mar, American Society of Composers, Authors and Publishers?"

"I guess."

"They have a complicated formula for how members get paid royalties. There's a sort of pyramid; the more songs you write and publish, the more royalties accrue to you. At the top of the pyramid one songwriter sits alone—at least he did for years, it's possible someone has replaced him now—Irving Berlin. He wrote 'What'll I Do?' "

Marlon was in and out of awareness; my words weren't to stimulate conversation, they were a lullaby for my friend.

"This cough," he said. "If I could control it, I could stop the shit problem. The area around my asshole is orange flames."

"Mar, there are gels that will numb that. I'll go down and get some, there's no reason to suffer from that skin that's gotten so sensitive. Or your doctor can prescribe something."

"It's diaper rash, that's what it is," he said.

"Right, so I'll go get something."

"Wait." He reached to the phone, it was an effort, he hit the intercom button and told Vee to have Angela call him, he wanted her to pick up something at the drugstore.

"Some life, eh?" he said, and paused. "I'm glad you came, Georgie. This'll get better. If it doesn't, fuck it, let it come, I don't care."

There it was again. Fuck death. No last-minute breakdown, no sudden sense of Nearer My God to Thee, no weeping. Marlon was consistent right to the end. Fuck death was something he'd said often before, but this time it came with a weariness, a simplicity that made it real.

We talked for another hour or so, Marlon's wakefulness dwindling. It seemed to me that an unearthly game of Steal the Flag was being played. Marlon's eyes close and death races farther into his body; his eyes open and death slows to a halt.

There were longer pauses; it seemed increasingly difficult for Marlon to hold the threads of contact. I'd been there nearly three hours, it was time to go.

"I'll call tomorrow, Mar. I'll come back the day after."

"Great, Georgie." He raised his head, his eyes made an effort to find mine. When they did, his gaze was steadfast and sober.

"I'm glad we got it all put back together." He said it simply and with his heart.

He lay back and was quiet. We were together again, Marlon and George in their old way, and that was all that was necessary.

I stood and took hold of his bare leg

With his eyes closed, he said softly, "I don't want you to touch me, Georgie, I'm covered with germs, I don't want you to take them back to Graves."

I massaged his leg for a moment, gave it a final loving squeeze, and left.

Angela had returned and she walked me to the car.

"I'd better come back tomorrow or the next day," I said. "This looks serious."

"Yes, but I think things are improving, he has a better battery of doctors now."

"Let me know if anything changes, if he starts to dip."

"Yes, of course."

The next evening at ten to seven, Vee called. "Mr. Englund,

I have some sad news. Mr. Brando passed away at six-twenty, just a little while ago."

A cry came out of me, the kind you don't know you're making. I said something to Vee, I don't remember what.

"Yes. I know he was glad you came," Vee said. "You were the last one to see him."

Marlon didn't want to die without us being together one last time. Once we were, he could let go. After all these years, it had come down to this.

And, sadly, this—all through his life Marlon did things the way they'd never been done before. But when it came to dying, his defiance of authority, his ability to improvise could not slow the corrosion inside him. One can guess at what imaginative exit Marlon might have concocted had he had the choice. But he didn't have a choice; he was obliged to leave this life the way everybody else does after a long illness, weary, in pain, and in submission.

In the first days after his death, the summings-up of his life and career are everywhere in newspapers and on television. He is accorded the signal place in acting history he merits. Every laudatory word about him is deserved.

Then comes the chin-stroking wisdom doled out by cinema mavens who tell us, though they never met him, that Marlon was mysterious, an outsider, rebellious, and perhaps the greatest actor of the century—though he squandered his talent in his last years. A well-known magazine critic who knew Marlon not at all pontificates about him. The host of a TV show about actors, who knows even less about Marlon, is queried and responds with bald effrontery, as if he actually did know something. These and their ilk pretend—or in their sage postures encourage the presumption—that they possess genuine knowledge of Marlon. Of course they don't.

The one thing they say in chorus, and it's true beyond doubt, is that Marlon was a private man. Yes, he was private and they were never, even for a moment, allowed behind the veil of that privacy. Why can't they say that? Why can't they say, "I can critique Brando's work, but I know positively nothing about the man himself"? Instead they mouth the gossip-alleged-to-be-gospel that has for years been passed around campfires as knowledge of Marlon.

A smile comes to my face as I imagine Marlon and me watching these shows together. He would fasten first on the man's dyed mustache, be curious that nobody told the creature how ersatz it looked. Then he would focus not so much on the total lack of substance in what the man was saying as on his preening that he had some relevance to the life of the now-dead Marlon Brando.

I'm experiencing this phenomenon in my own life. People from the periphery whom I've known only casually, others I have neither seen nor talked to in years, call and almost religiously use the same phrase: "I just want you to know I'm thinking about you." Some, feigning a sympathy they cannot possibly feel, mouth the even more intrusive, "How are you doing?" As if there were a coherent answer to that question and I would be happy to share my scattered, sorrowful thoughts with them.

To call this insincerity would not be wholly accurate, but there is no question that much of the motivation comes from the feeling that just making the call gives them proximity to the event of Marlon's death. Around a celebrity death like this, a special species of bird appears in faux black plumage and pecks for bits that might in some way associate it with this passing.

It is late at night and I am alone in what Shelley called "a sad satiety," all is silent. There should be a symphony playing that was written for Marlon. A symphony by Mahler because he wrote so well the music of complexity, he pained you, pounded you, then released an underground melody of such purity and hope as to carry you into life again. Next, a poet laureate should recite a flowing elegy to Marlon. I do not have that elegy in me; all light and beauty have gone somewhere else. I am empty at last, devoid finally of thought and emotion.

Yet, into the emptiness, the wide, silent world of loss, comes a fragment from a country-western song I know.

> These feet will do the walking
> But you must do the talking
> 'Cause these lips don't know how to say goodbye.

They don't, Mar, I can't get them to shape the word.